Trauma Debriefing Handbook
for Schools and Agencies

William Steele, MSW, PsyD

ISBN 1-931310-03-3

The National Institute for Trauma and Loss in Children
900 Cook Road
Grosse Pointe Woods, MI 48236

www.tlcinstitute.org

TLC is a program of Children's Home of Detroit

A Program of
Children's Home
of Detroit

**The National Institute for
Trauma and Loss in Children**
900 Cook Road
Grosse Pointe Woods, MI 48236
1-877-306-5256 Toll-free

www.tlcinstitute.org

Visit TLC's web site for information about:

- **grief and trauma in children, adolescence, and adults**
- **parent trauma resources**
- **school and clinical resources**
- **TLC trainings, intervention programs, and resource materials**

About the Author
and the
The National Institute for Trauma and Loss in Children

William Steele, MSW, PsyD Founder and Director of TLC

Established in 1990, The National Institute for Trauma and Loss in Children (TLC) is the outcome of Dr. Steele's involvement with helping schools across the country develop crisis response teams in the early 1980's to deal with the epidemic of suicide among young people. When violence emerged as the new epidemic in the late 1980's, so too came the long needed acknowledgement that children do in fact experience Post-traumatic Stress Disorder (PTSD). Today, we know that exposure to both violent and non-violent incidents can induce PTSD in children. Murder, suicide, physical/sexual assault, domestic violence, house fires, car fatalities, drownings, critical injuries, terminal illness, surgeries, divorce, foster placement, community and natural disasters have all led to the need for trauma-specific training, resource materials and intervention programs specific to traumatized children. TLC fills this need.

Dr. Steele has assisted over 1,500 school districts in developing or upgrading their crisis response teams. He continues to actively consult and provide debriefing to those exposed to critical, trauma inducing incidents. He has presented to over 40,000 educators and human service professionals nationally and was one of the first Americans selected by the Kuwait government after the Gulf War to train their newly formed mental health staff. He is the author of many programs and publications, most recently, *Structured Sensory Intervention for Children, Adolescents and Parents (SITCAP)*. He established the Certification Program for Trauma and Loss School Specialist, Trauma and Loss Consultant, and Trauma and Loss Consultant Supervisor and is responsible for the development of several trauma-specific intervention programs. He is the author of the *Trauma Response Intervention Program: Short Term Intervention Model* (Steele and Raider, 2001) field-tested by 120 professionals who provided over 2,400 individual interventions for traumatized children. Today, there are over 4,000 TLC Certified Trauma and Loss School Specialists, Consultants, and Consultant supervisors across the country.

As an educator, social worker and psychologist Dr. Steele has integrated both clinical and educational models of intervention into TLC resource materials and specialized programs that are practical, timely and designed for use in both school and agency settings. He is most proud of the 300+ professionals who have given countless hours of their time field-testing and fine tuning the programs and resource materials developed by TLC. Field-testing, ensures the usability and adaptability in both school and agency settings and documents the programs benefit to the traumatized children they are designed to help.

What others say about TLC...

"I will put to use what I've learned immediately!"
Jane King, Elementary Counselor, Bainbridge, Indiana

"Excellent hands-on, practical interventions and TLC is always available for consultation!"
Barbara Brunkan, Social Worker, Davenport, Iowa

"Tremendous job...my ten districts are now working together on our crisis response following traumatic events."
Regional Superintendent, Rock Island, Illinois

"Structured and tested, TLC gets to the heart of the problems."
Patti Porter, Counselor, Tyler, Texas

"Very focused, direct, practical strategies at a time when managed health care calls for measurable outcomes."
Kennedy Krieger Family Center, Baltimore, Maryland

"Effective, practical, flexible, cost effective and easy to use."
Leena K. Singh, Counselor, Sarnia, Ontario, Canada

"Invaluable in helping children talk about their painful and terrifying experiences."
Donna Groth, Social Worker, Detroit, Michigan

"A program that comes from people who work in the trenches is so welcomed!"
Cathy Wunderlich, Counselor, Silvis, Illinois

**Special Thanks to the
John S. and James L. Knight Foundation
whose support has made this Handbook and video tape possible.**

To get a referral or find out more information, please call TLC toll-free at
877-306-5256 or visit www.tlcinstitute.org.

Contents

Acknowledgements

A special thank you to Noreen and Paul Brohl for the hours they spent editing this handbook. Their input has greatly contributed to make this an easy to use, practical tool.

Thanks also to all the TLC Consultants and School Specialists whose questions, comments and feedback shaped the content and design of this handbook to meet the varied intervention needs of schools and agencies following trauma inducing incidents.

Additional thanks to my son, Officer Darren Steele and Officer Bob Rabe, for sharing their knowledge of and experience with critical incident stress debriefing.

I would like to identify all of you who helped develop this handbook, but the list would be too long. So, thank you very much to all of the participants from Michigan, Illinois, Indiana, Texas, Iowa, Ohio, Pennsylvania and Canada. Your feedback has been invaluable.

Why This Handbook?

* The Debriefing Model proposed in this Handbook is a variation of the original model of Jeffrey Mitchell used following disasters - Critical Incident Stress Debriefing (CISD). CISD is now referred to as Critical Incident Stress Management (CISM) to better reflect the various processes related to debriefing.

* CISD was originally used to assist medical, emergency, law enforcement and rescue personnel involved in treating survivors, and searching for victims of major disasters.

* The CISD Model was not originally designed for use in school and agency settings with staff, students and clients of all ages.

* The growing number of traumas faced by schools and agencies has led to the need for responses similar to CISD, but adapted to school and agency settings.

* Unfortunately, attempts to integrate debriefing components into a crisis response in school and agency settings have led to many variations which are not always based upon a clear understanding of the purpose for, and use of, debriefing techniques.

* Trauma Debriefing in schools and agencies is designed specifically for use in schools, mental health, and child and family service agencies following traumatic incidents involving staff, students or clients.

* Distinctions among Trauma Debriefing, Operational Debriefing, Defusing, and Classroom Presentations are clearly defined.

* Six types of trauma debriefing have been designed to be used in schools and agencies. Trauma Debriefing, Defusing, Classroom Presentations, Operational Debriefing, Debriefing Crisis Teams and Individual Debriefing specifically address the different needs of the students and clients of various ages, the distinct needs of the most-exposed and least-exposed staff, and the distinct needs of the crisis team members. Likewise, they address the needs of all staff in relationship to the system in which they must perform during the crisis. Finally, they address the informational and educational needs of students and clients which are outside the realm of debriefing and defusing.

a

* *Trauma Debriefing For Schools and Agencies* answers the one hundred most commonly asked questions asked by school and agency personnel related to its use, benefits and risks.

* The Handbook provides the scripts for each of its models, handout materials for participants, checklists, and additional supportive materials.

* The models presented and recommended for integration into existing crisis response teams protocols are the direct result of the frontline experience of 3,000 professionals, who have participated in the trainings provided by The National Institute for Trauma and Loss in Children (TLC).

* Hundreds of school districts and a growing number of community mental health centers, child and family agencies, organizations and programs are now assisting one another with the debriefing, defusing strategies presented in this handbook.

* Although the handbook provides you with a comprehensive overview of the debriefing process and specific stage-by-stage scripting, we do recommend training prior to the use of the strategies presented. Competency is greatly enhanced when you can first see how an intervention works and then practice it before implementing it.

b

DEBRIEFING MODELS

DEBRIEFING	DEFUSING	OPERATIONAL
FOR WHOM		
• reserved for most-exposed students (5th - 6th grade and up) and staff	• reserved for most-exposed children K - 5th grade	• appropriate for entire staff
WHEN		
• initiated three days to two weeks after event (even months later is appropriate) • follow up debriefing 4-6 weeks after the incident	• initiated three days to one week after the event • follow up 2-6 weeks after initial debriefing	• initiated first day • follow up in three-to-five days. Thereafter, as determined by duration of event
SIZE		
• limit to 8-10 participants per group	• can be conducted with most-exposed class (limit to 8-10 students)	• any number
CONDUCTED BY		
• three debriefers (can be crisis team members)	• two to four debriefers depending upon size of group and age	• outside consultant
DURATION		
• two hours	• 30 minutes to one hour	• one hour
PURPOSES		
• to mitigate impact of event • to accelerate healing • to identify what happened • what role participants played • what cognitive behavioral & emotional reactions were experienced • to educate about signs & symptoms • to normalize • to identify related issues, support needed • to summarize and prepare for next several days, weeks, months • to refer as needed	• includes all the purposes of debriefing NOTE: We now recommend *Helping Children Feel Safe* sensory activities the first two days followed by the formal debriefing model with the most exposed 3-5 days following exposure. (See Appendix I)	• to evaluate current status of staff and students/clients • to share new information and clarify rumors • to determine additional needs for immediate resources and support • to prepare staff for possible upcoming problems • to help staff care for themselves • to reinforce positive aspects emerging from this event
FORMAT		
• question, answer, inform	• question, answer, inform, drawing, story telling, reading, other activities.	• question, answer, inform

d

DEBRIEFING MODELS

DEBRIEFING TEAMS	CLASSROOM PRESENTATION
FOR WHOM	
• crisis team members	• appropriate for all grades
WHEN	
• within two weeks	• initiate immediately - within first week
SIZE	
• limit to no more than 10	• entire classroom participation
CONDUCTED BY	
• outside consultant	• crisis team - one-two members or teachers and team members
DURATION	
• one to two hours	• 30 - 45 minutes • one time presentation
PURPOSES	
• to help process difficult personal reactions • to identify procedures within the system which helped or hindered effective interventions • to evaluate each member's performance and overall team performance • prepare for future incidents	• to gather information on students reactions, questions, concerns, information about event and victim(s) • to provide factual information to minimize rumors, misperceptions • to normalize current reactions • to educate as to possible future reactions and what students can do and where they can go for help • to identify appropriate behavior in the midst of such a crisis • to encourage students to ask for help if needed/referral • to inform of upcoming related activities e.g. memorial service
FORMAT	
• question, answer, explore, problem solve	• question, answer, inform, problem solve

Debriefing Models

e

f

The Questions You Ask:
The Handbook Answers

Debriefing: What is it?

What is debriefing?
What is its purpose?
What are its objectives?
What are the differences between trauma intervention and debriefing?
Does debriefing work?
What kind of incidents might call for debriefing?
How does debriefing fit into already existing crisis response teams?
What are the differences between grief and trauma?
What are some common trauma reactions?
How do trauma reactions differ from acute stress?
Is debriefing effective with complex PTSD victims?

Who and When?

Who gets debriefed?
Who decides who gets debriefed?
Can an individual be debriefed?
When is the best time to initiate debriefing?
How long after an incident can a debriefing be conducted?
How long does a debriefing session take?
How many people can be debriefed at one time?
Should administrators/supervisors be included in the group with line staff?
Can debriefing be provided to participants (professionals) who have been exposed to different traumas at different times?
Can we have more than one session with the same people in one day?
Can we debrief the same people several times over an extended period?
If we were to offer to return for debriefing with the same group what might be the optimum time to conduct a follow up session?
Would the same process be used at this follow up session?

How and What Do We Need?

How many debriefers are needed to conduct a debriefing?
Who can be a debriefer in school and agency settings?
Are there times or factors that might indicate that a debriefer not debrief?
Are there ground rules?
Should law enforcement representatives provide factual information to the group prior to starting the debriefing in those cases where there is police involvement?
What do we do with those participants who have been told by police not to talk about details because of an ongoing investigation?
Can we be subpoenaed to testify - reveal information shared in the debriefing?
What about confidentiality?
When debriefing children, what additional concerns about confidentiality exist?
What do we say to participants about phone calls, beepers, being called out of the meeting to attend to students, clients or administrative issues?
How should the room be set up?
What props do we need for debriefing sessions?
Is it okay to have refreshments?
What kind of handout materials should we have available?
What procedure needs to be in place prior to starting a session in order to appropriately begin and end the session?

Debriefing Stages

What are the debriefing stages?
How do we get started?
What do we ask about initially?
Can we use our own words when asking questions?
If there are multiple victims how do we ask participants about their relationship to the victims?
Do debriefers have a script?
Do we take notes to document the session?
Do we always go in the same order of asking questions?
What happens when a debriefer neglects to ask one of the questions - does another debriefer jump in and ask?
When is it appropriate to ask for clarification, to reflect, to normalize reactions?
Is it appropriate to ask multiple questions of participants?

Responding to Participants

What if someone doesn't want to talk?
How do we respond to a participant who answers our questions with "I don't know"?
What if someone doesn't want to stop talking?
What if someone gets so upset he gets up to leave?
What is our responsibility to the person who leaves?
Who else should be available to assist in this situation?
What liabilities might be in question?
What do we tell the rest of the participants?
Could this person return to the debriefing?
Which debriefers should be prepared to handle this type of situation?
What do we do if a participant does not actually answer the question asked?
How do we handle blame and anger?
What do we do when participants bring up policy, procedural, staffing, administrative issues specific to the incident?
What do we do when participants begin to comfort one another with hugs?
In the summary stage is it critical to reference responses heard from each of the participants?
What is one of the major considerations to be addressed in the summary stage unique to school and agency settings?
How do you initiate a discussion about the positive factors that have emerged from their experiences?

At Risk Participants

What are the issues when there is a concern for a potentially at risk participant?
Who is ultimately responsible for that persons safety?
What tools exist to evaluate for PTSD?
If someone needs individual attention what do we do?
How do we determine the severity of a participants reactions?
When do we refer a participant for additional treatment?
Are there characteristics which distinguish victims from survivors?
What if a participant is talking about suicide?
What if people need more assistance after debriefing/defusing sessions. What type of intervention is recommended?

Debriefer Concerns

What happens if one of us (debriefer) becomes visually upset?
What are the transference and countertransference (vicarious traumatization) issues debriefers must be aware of as a debriefer?
Are there special issues to address when debriefing the debriefers?
Do already existing crisis team members act as debriefers for their own staff?
Can we debrief ourselves?
What shouldn't we do immediately following the end of a debriefing session?

Defusing/Classrooms

Can you debrief a classroom?
How is defusing different than debriefing?
What are the goals of defusing?
What age level is appropriate for the defusing process?
What are the stages of defusing?
How long does a defusing session run?
If we are defusing a group of children related to a murder, how do you generalize murder?
Is there anyone who should not be in a defusing session?
Is there a good book to read to younger children that speaks directly to trauma?
How large can a defusing group be and still allow for an effective intervention?

Operational Debriefing

How do we debrief an entire school or agency staff?
What are the goals of Operational Debriefing?
What are the purposes of Operational Debriefing?
How much time should we plan to take?
What do we do with administrators?
What specific questions would we ask when conducting this type of debriefing?
Are handout materials different for this group than those given in smaller sessions with the most-exposed victims?
How many debriefers are needed for Operational Debriefing sessions and who should conduct it?

Chapter One
What Is Debriefing?

What is debriefing?

Petersen and Straub (1994) define debriefing as "the process of putting the incident (trauma) and the individual's reactions in perspective." Johnson (1993) specifically describes debriefing as "a form of crisis intervention...individuals can air their perceptions of the event, their reactions to it, and their concerns for the future in a structured, supportive context." Mitchell (1991 CISD Video) defines debriefing as "a group process designed to mitigate the impact of the event and to accelerate normal recovery." Meichenbaum (1994) describes debriefing as "a group method that helps the workers to process and defuse their emotional reactions by means of educational, preventative, and supportive process. It is designed to prevent unnecessary complications that follow from exposure to disasters."

Debriefing dates back to the early 1900's when it was used in the military. Mitchell is credited with adapting military protocol to fit the needs of emergency health care workers and rescue personnel. In the 1970's he titled his model *Critical Incident Stress Debriefing* (CISD). Today, his Critical Incident Stress Management (CISM) includes crisis intervention as part of the process.

Other models have been developed since the CISD model. Armstrong (1991), Griffin (1987), Raphael (1986), and Wagner (1979) have all developed models, but Mitchell's model receives the most attention.

The Mitchell CISD process has been altered by others for adaptation in school settings as well. Petersen and Straub (1994) for example, recommended that no more than fifteen - twenty people be debriefed at one time. They identify five phases of the process. Johnson (1993) suggests that up to 40 students can be debriefed at one time with the basic rule of "take as long as it takes" to complete. He identifies five stages to the process as well, which were adapted from Mitchell's seven stage model.

The model attached in this handbook is far more specific and structured than most. It is based upon our critical incident experiences dating back to the early 1980's when the epidemic of suicide among young people resulted in the development of crisis response teams.

What are it's objectives?

Debriefing is a group intervention process whose objectives are: to provide participants the opportunity to share information related to the details of the incident; to identify the cognitive, behavioral, emotional, and physical reactions to it; to alter, as needed, perceptions and understanding of the incident and reactions to it; to find some relief from the experience via participant support, normalization of reactions and corrections of misperceptions; and to prepare participants for reactions they might experience in the future; and to suggest ways they can cope with current and possible future reactions.

This approach addresses specific needs and limitations of school and agency settings. It provides models for debriefing, defusing, classroom presentations and administrative (operational) debriefings. Each of these differences will be discussed in the handbook.

What is its purpose?

The purpose of debriefing is to accelerate healing from the terror induced by traumatic incidents and to prevent the formation of Posttraumatic Stress Disorder (PTSD).

How does debriefing fit into existing Crisis Response Teams?

Debriefing fits naturally into the overall activities of existing crisis response teams in school settings. Crisis teams are designed to respond immediately to all in need. The majority of schools with crisis teams generally have been trained to conduct assessments, meet with students, assist teachers with classroom presentations and provide crisis intervention as needed. Many, however, have not been trained in debriefing techniques. Some students and staff will be more in need than others. Debriefing is a process that works well with those most in need and the most-exposed - those who are surviving victims, witnesses to the incident or related to the victim(s), such as family members, close friends, teacher, coach.

Members of the crisis teams should be trained in debriefing techniques. This process is very different from staffing a "grieving room" or sitting with a group of students and asking them what they are feeling or thinking. It is different from attempting to assist a classroom of forty students.

The one debriefing function that crisis team members cannot do, is debrief themselves. It is very helpful for schools today to have a relationship with professionals outside the school system who have debriefing experiences.

Not only do we advise crisis team members not to debrief themselves, we also suggest they not attempt to debrief their own staff. Objectivity is difficult enough to maintain in the middle of a crisis. It is even more difficult with people we work with or relate to on a daily basis.

A crisis response team protocol needs to include the debriefing of most-exposed students by team members, and the debriefing of the team members and staff by debriefers outside the school. These could be district-wide crisis team members or those professionals trained in debriefing who work in the community and are known to the school system.

What type of incident requires debriefing?

Debriefing is generally applied to those situations which induce acute stress. By definition this would be sudden, unexpected, unusual human experience. The incident would have posed a serious threat to one's life or physical integrity, or to the life of a family member or close friend or to one's surrounding environment (home, school, workplace). This would also include those individuals who were witnesses to such an incident.

TLC's research (Raider, Santiago & Steele, 1998) found high levels of trauma severity in children exposed to murder, suicide, domestic violence, physical/sexual abuse, car fatalities, house fires, drowning, critical injuries due to environmental tragedies or accidents, terminal illness, separation from a parent, divorce, living with substance abusing parents, etc.

The research also found high levels of trauma following life threatening incidents such as floods, hurricanes, workplace violence, community violence, explosions, fires, overturned school buses, hostage situations, kidnappings, suicides, and other sudden deaths. All of these incidents could require debriefing.

Hobfoll (1994) has designed a model in which he identifies four sources of stress arising from a disaster: a) objects, b) conditions, c) personal characteristics, d) energies.

Objects involve the loss of our personal possessions. At a personal level, this could include the loss of our car, home, etc.; and at a community level, less access to roads, shelters, emergency equipment, etc.

Conditions which can be lost at a personal level could include our social ties and roles (employment, parenthood, marriage) and at the community level - the loss of the opportunity to work, to secure emergency services, etc.

Personal characteristics which can be lost include the inner strengths of the individual, e.g. self-esteem, self-efficacy and those "outer" attributes which reflect inner strengths e.g. social skills, specialized work skills, etc. At a community level such characteristics could include community pride and competence.

Energies at a personal level refer to resources such as money, food, knowledge, etc. At a community level these refer to community resources such as money, transportation, safety, how the community (at a government level) responds to a crisis.

This model reminds us that a trauma can be created not only from our involvement with the specific incident itself, but also through the additional losses it can create for us at a personal and community level.

It is important to keep in mind, however, that it is not the incident itself which induces acute stress, but the level of vulnerability and powerlessness of the child, or adult, at the time of the incident which can leave him exposed to posttraumatic stress.

What are the differences between grief and trauma, acute stress, posttraumatic stress?

There are significant differences between grief and trauma, acute stress and Posttraumatic Stress Disorder.

Debriefing generally is reserved for trauma victims who are experiencing acute stress. To appreciate the debriefing process it is important to understand the differences between grief and trauma and then the differences between acute stress and Posttraumatic Stress Disorder (PTSD).

Following is a chart comparing grief and trauma differences. It is easy to see that at the core of trauma is terror. When we are in terror, everything feels chaotic and out of control. A structured debriefing process is designed to minimize the chaos and help participants regain a sense of control over the chaos and terror.

GRIEF	TRAUMA
Generalized reaction is SADNESS	Generalized reaction is TERROR
Grief reactions stand alone	Trauma reactions generally include grief reactions
Grief reactions are generally known to the public and the professional	Trauma reactions especially in children are largely unknown to the public and often professionals
In grief, most can generally talk about what happened	In trauma, most do not want to talk about what happened
In grief, pain is the acknowledgement of the loss	In trauma, pain triggers tremendous terror and an overwhelming sense of powerlessness and loss of safety
In grief, anger is generally non-destructive and non-assaultive	In trauma, anger often becomes assaultive even after non-violent trauma
In grief, guilt says "I wish I would/would not have…"	Trauma guilt says, "It was my fault. I could have prevented it" and "It should have been me instead."
Grief generally does not attack nor "disfigure" our self image	Trauma generally attacks, distorts and "disfigures" our self image
In grief, dreams tend to be of the deceased	In trauma, dreams are about self as potential victim
Grief generally does not involve trauma reactions like flashbacks, startle reactions, hypervigilance, numbing, etc.	Trauma involves grief reactions in addition to trauma-specific reactions we have discussed

Acute Stress Period - Four Weeks

The time when most individuals will experience acute stress reactions is within the first four weeks following a critical incident. It is during this time that debriefing is used to prevent the onset of Posttraumatic Stress Disorder (PTSD).

PTSD Period - Four Weeks After

Posttraumatic Stress reactions are the same as acute stress reactions. The only difference is that once acute stress reactions continue beyond the initial four week period, or additional reactions emerge beyond that four week period (delayed response), the diagnosis of PTSD is likely. Once an individual moves to PTSD additional trauma-specific intervention is critical. Debriefing is the process that many believe can help prevent PTSD from taking hold.

REEXPERIENCING	PERSISTENT AVOIDANCE	INCREASED AROUSAL
• Intrusive thoughts, feelings • Traumatic dreams • Flashbacks • Intense psychological distress triggered by reminders • Physiological reactivity	• Of thoughts, feelings, talking of activities, places, people associated with trauma • Inability to recall • Numbing, detachment, estrangement • Restricted affect • Foreshortened future	• Sleep difficulty • Irritability, assaultive behavior • Difficulty concentrating • Difficulty remembering • Hypervigilance • Startle response

Acute Stress - PTSD Reactions

PTSD is the diagnosis when these reactions persist or develop four weeks beyond the initial incident and when there exists one or more reexperiencing reactions; three or more avoidance reactions and two or more arousal reactions.

Steele, (1997) provides a descriptive definition of acute stress - PTSD reactions for children.

PTSD Reactions in Children

* **Cognitive dysfunction involving memory and learning.** "A" students become "C" students; severe reactions cause others to fail altogether.

* **Inability to concentrate.** Children who once could complete two and three different tasks now have difficulty with a single task. Parents and educators often react negatively to this behavior because they simply do not understand its cause.

* **Tremendous fear and anxiety.** One seventeen-month-old boy who witnessed his father kill his mother is now seven-years-old. He still sleeps on the floor, ever ready to run from danger. Six-year-old Elizabeth, whose sister was killed one year earlier, is also sleeping on the floor. She did not witness her sister's murder, yet she is experiencing this same hypervigilant PTSD response.

Increased aggression, fighting, assaultive behavior - these are the first reactions generally identified as a change since the trauma. Revenge is a constant theme when the incident has been a violent one. Other reactions may include:

* **Survivor guilt**: Students not in school at the time of a random shooting and subsequent death of a fellow student feel accountable and experience intrusive thoughts and images. Another form of survivor guilt is the belief that "It should have been me instead" or "I wish it would have been me instead."

* **Intrusive images** (flashbacks): Two years later, teachers still notice this teenage girl engaging in a plucking motion with her hand. She was home when the beating occurred. She did not know her mother was already dead when she ran to help her. When she rolled her mother over, her mother's mouth was filled with blood and broken teeth. The daughter began pulling the broken teeth from her mother's mouth so she wouldn't choke on them. Two years later, that plucking motion still occurred when she's reexperiencing her experience.

* **Traumatic dreams**: Eleven-year-old Tommy was a survivor, not a witness, when we first met him one year after his sister was killed by a serial killer. He was still having dreams of his "guts" being ripped out by "Candyman." His sister had been stabbed repeatedly in the chest/stomach area.

* **Inappropriate age-related behavior**: These include clinging to mother, enuresis, and other regressive behaviors. Eleven-year-old Tommy, the boy mentioned above, has started to stutter.

* **Startle reactions**: After her father beat her mother to death, the police arrived to take pictures and arrest the father. Two years later, this daughter still cannot allow her picture to be taken because it reminds her of that day.

* **Emotional detachment**: Fifteen-year-old Mary, whose sister was also killed by a serial killer, had made friends her mother described as "real trouble." She never even cried at the funeral. She had received help, but not the trauma-specific help we provided her later.

Behaviorally children may exhibit the following:

* Trouble sleeping, being afraid to sleep alone even for short periods of time

* Be easily startled (terrorized) by sounds, sights, smells similar to those that existed at the time of the event - a car backfiring may sound like the gun shot that killed someone; for one child, his dog pouncing down the stairs brought back the sound of his father falling down the stairs and dying

* Become hypervigilant - forever watching out for and anticipating that they are about to be or are in danger

* Seek safety "spots" in their environment, in whatever room they may be in at the time. Children who sleep on the floor instead of their bed after a trauma do so because they fear the comfort of a bed will let them sleep so hard that they won't hear danger coming

* Become irritable, aggressive, act tough, provoke fights

* Verbalize a desire for revenge

* Act as if they are no longer afraid of anything or anyone verbalizing that nothing ever scares them anymore and in the face of danger, respond inappropriately.

* Forget recently acquired skills

* Return to behaviors they had previously stopped, i.e. bed-wetting, nail-biting, or developing disturbing behaviors such as stuttering

* Withdraw and want to do less with their friends

* Develop physical complaints: headaches, stomach problems, fatigue, and other ailments not previously present

* Become accident prone, taking risks they had previously avoided, putting themselves in life threatening situations, reenacting the event as a victim or a hero

* Developing a pessimistic view of the future, losing their resilience to overcome additional difficulties, losing hope, losing their passion to survive, play, and enjoy life

Adults may express Acute Stress\PTSD with the following behaviors (Johnson, 1993).

* Seems disconnected/preoccupied
* Not as neat in dress and habits
* Late, many absences, fatigued
* Low morale, change of attitude toward work
* Avoids certain situations/places
* Talks compulsively or not at all about incident
* Irritable, conflicts with others, and possibly with you
* Drinking, drug use
* Sudden change in lifestyle
* Aches, pains, illnesses
* Unhappiness, dissatisfaction

Lenore Terr (1991) makes a distinction between Type I and Type II Trauma. Type I Trauma refers to those incidents which are short term and unexpected. Usually these are one time incidents of limited duration and could include rape, natural disasters, car accidents, etc.

Type II Trauma are sustained and repeated exposure to a series of events or exposure to a single prolonged event. Repeated abuse, is an example of singular, prolonged, but repeated exposure. Type II Traumas frequently lead to long term interpersonal and characterological problems or to complex PTSD reactions when left untreated.

Does debriefing work?

Clinical experience has shown that debriefing accelerates healing and lessens the severity of symptoms. In general, participants are immensely grateful for the opportunity to share the details of their ordeal, to listen to the experience of others, discover they are not alone in their reactions, and to learn that what they are experiencing is normal.

In my own experience, there is no doubt that debriefing helps accelerate healing, restores inner control and order, and provides relief from stress.

Actual research always lags behind clinical experiences. This certainly does not invalidate the process. There have been very few studies to document the impact of debriefing on trauma victims. Definitive conclusions are not possible due to sample size and the variety of debriefing processes. Despite these limitations, findings do suggest that debriefing can reduce trauma reactions.

Yule (1992) studied the impact of debriefing on survivors of the Jupiter Cruise Ship sinking in 1988. Two seamen, one teacher and one pupil were killed when the Jupiter was sunk by a tanker. There were 400 children and 90 teachers aboard. Many had to jump into the sea. Nearly half of the surviving children experienced PTSD. They ranged in age from 11-18-years-old with most being between 14-15-years-old. Debriefing was held ten days after the incident. Thereafter, two small groups were run. Problem solving strategies were added to the debriefing model to deal with anxiety, avoidance and intrusive thoughts. The children involved in the early intervention showed a reduction in symptoms nine months later. The problem with this study, however, was that debriefing was not the only intervention provided.

Shalev (1994), Raphel et al. (1994), suggest that there is little systematic evidence such as controlled studies, or long-term follow-up to support the benefits of debriefing. In fact, McFarlane (1994) notes that "The few outcome studies of debriefing, which have comparison groups, suggest that these interventions may worsen the outcome of some of those participating rather than having the desired effect of lessening the distress of those involved."

McFarlane does go on to say that this concern must be placed alongside the strong perceptions that debriefing is helpful. Understanding that simple exposure to hearing of the details (Saigh, 1991) can induce trauma one might expect an increase at least temporarily in stress levels and symptomatology. It is also important to understand that delayed reactions may account for this "worsening," not the debriefing itself. There is no way to predict who will or will not benefit from debriefing.

Pynoos (1994) reported the reduction of severe reactions in two classes of Armenian students involved in an earthquake. In addition to debriefing, students received 3-4 individual and group sessions over the next year and a half after the earthquake. Almost 92% of the children experienced a significant reduction in their trauma symptoms, which was said to be remarkable, because of the "unremitting severity" of the disaster. However, because debriefing was not the only intervention used, it is impossible to draw conclusions about the effectiveness of debriefing by itself.

Debriefing: Criticism – Response

Following 9/11 articles emerged "debunking" debriefing and indicated that debriefing could, in fact, be dangerous for participants and that not-talking for many can be a healthier way to recover from or manage the reactions related to exposure. However, research does exist to support the process and when closely evaluated, criticism is focused on one aspect of the process rather than the total process (Everly, G., Mitchell, I., 2000; Mitchell, J., 2004).

No one intervention fits every individual. Yes, some do heal on their own, while others need help. Debriefing should be, for this reason, completed voluntarily; not mandated by administrators or health care professionals. The choice was not always available to participants following 9/11. This was inappropriate and, in some cases, bordered on unethical practices for pay.

The reality is that any intervention used inappropriately becomes a dangerous intervention. Debriefing was never intended as a same-day response. In fact, debriefing should not be conducted for at least three (3) or four (4) days after exposure. Victims need time to process their experience, to get past the initial shock and disbelief. For many, the first few days are a time when victims just cannot think. If children are the participants parental permission is mandatory and debriefing needs to be a combination of cognitive and sensory activities.

This entire text is devoted to setting boundaries and identifying the different types of debriefing processes based upon developmental readiness of participants. The reality is that there are numerous studies that do support the value of debriefing for the majority of participants who will participate. However, as with any intervention, professionals must be sensitive to, and trained to recognize those who are not feeling safe with the debriefing process presented and take ethical and professional responsibility to protect all participants.

Many participants of debriefing have supported its value to them. Perhaps its importance is the attention, education, and support these resources immediately provide victims. Experience tells us that participants are far more likely to accept intervention brought to them versus actually pursuing intervention on their own. And, when debriefing is provided professionally within the boundaries detailed in this text, the majority of participants will report that it was helpful.

What is the difference between debriefing and trauma-specific intervention?

Debriefing does not utilize trauma-specific intervention processes like guided imagery, drawing, art activities, hypnosis, use of metaphors, etc. Debriefing's purpose is to acknowledge, share, empathize, reassure, and support. The purpose of trauma intervention is to explore, search for personal insight and meaning, focus on past trauma inducing memories triggered by the most recent event and take the time needed to work through the most troubling issues triggered by the trauma experience. Debriefers act as a referral source for those needing intervention beyond the initial debriefing period. They are not necessarily clinically trained in psychology, social work or other graduate level clinical areas.

Chapter Two
Who and When?

Who gets debriefed?

To understand who may need debriefing, it is critical to understand how we can become exposed to acute stress - PTSD reactions.

Exposure: There are four possible avenues of exposure, 1) as surviving victim - victims of physical/sexual abuse, other assaults, community violence, critical injuries, catastrophic situations, etc., 2) as witness to any potential trauma inducing incident violent or non-violent - murder, suicide, assault, car fatality, bus tragedy, house fire, drowning, etc., 3) being related to the victim - as a family member, friend, or peer. "Relationship" may also include one's personal identification with victims. (Schwarz (1991) study of 64 children following a school shooting showed that irrespective of physical nearness to the event, emotional stress resulting from personal identification also led to PTSD); 4) Verbal exposure - Saigh (1991) found that listening to the details of traumatic experiences, traumatic stress reactions can be induced. This is especially true for professionals responsible for intervention with traumatized children. Vicarious traumatization is always a potential development. Children who are exposed to repeated media coverage of details and survivors, understandably still may be exposed to prolonged and or more intense trauma reactions.

Being "related to" and a "witness to" is far more frequent in today's technological society. Approximately six months after the Oklahoma bombing this author was speaking to a group of Head Start teachers. During the presentation, one of the teachers told the story of how her children spontaneously devised a game where one half of them took all their sleeping (floor) mats and covered themselves. The other half in pairs of two, one at a time would go over to the other children, lift up the mat, pick up the child under the mat and then escort that child over to the other side of the room by their indoor soccer nets. They did this until all the children under the mats were rescued and taken to the "safety nets." Afterward, they switched sides. Rescuers became victims trapped under the mats; victims were now rescuers.

By being witnesses to the tragedies of the bombing and seeing the rescue workers carry out children their own ages from the rubble of their day care center, these children identified with the victims and consequently needed to find a way to conquer the fear induced by being witnesses and "related to" the victims.

Given the understanding of exposure we could say for example, that an entire school could need debriefing following a school bus accident, a suicide or some other critical incident. **There is no argument that all children will need attention, information, education and an opportunity to ask questions and talk about what happened. Not everyone will need to participate in the full debriefing process.**

A distinction needs to be made between "classroom presentation" and debriefing. Classroom presentations when conducted appropriately, provide the majority of students the information and opportunities they need to cope successfully with the school's experience. (This handbook devotes an entire section to the differences between classroom presentation and debriefing.)

Classroom presentations could be conducted for the entire student body immediately following the incident and then again to provide educational information related to the factors of the incident, ways to cope, etc.

Following a classroom presentation, those children who have been identified by their behavior as needing additional help would be seen individually. They could then be evaluated for level of risk, need for debriefing and need of further services.

Debriefing is reserved for the most-exposed. Initially, it includes those who witnessed the trauma or were surviving victims of the incident, were a family member or close friend of the victim or have a "perceived identity" with the victim. Others may be identified as needing debriefing but will initially need to be evaluated to determine what actually might be best for them. Keep in mind that debriefing is generally best initiated about 3-to-7 days following the incident where as classroom work can be done immediately.

Who decides who gets debriefed?

Many participants will be easy to identify as "most-exposed"- surviving victims, witnesses, family members or close friends. Survivors themselves will identify one another. Counselors, teachers, and administrators familiar with the victims will generally know of siblings or close friends who may be in need.

All staff members need to be aware of how they are to refer those in their care for help. Crisis teams can screen for appropriateness of debriefing. Administrators in agency settings may need to consult with an outside consultant. It would be appropriate for an outside consultant to provide administrators with guidelines for choosing those who may need formal debriefing.

14

Crisis team members can arrange appropriate groups and assign debriefing staff. Administrators of agencies need to be familiar with professionals/organizations with debriefing experience.

Can individuals be debriefed?

We strongly recommend that hesitant individuals be encouraged to attend the group process. The value and benefit of the group process is that participants are able to hear the reactions of others and, in listening, learn that their own experiences or reactions are quite normal and that they are not alone. This is far more difficult to accomplish individually. Sometimes it will be helpful to describe the process and let them know that they do not need to answer every question. However, if an individual is still reluctant, he should be provided individual attention.

Morten and Talbot (1990) have conducted individual debriefings in situations they suggest are not conducive to group debriefing such as following a bank robbery. The process would be no different except that one would think that the debriefer would take a more active role related to the affirmations, normalizations, etc. that would otherwise be forthcoming from participants in the group process. Due to the absence of feedback from group participants several individual sessions may be necessary.

The critical issue with individual debriefing is keeping a focus on the goal of debriefing and the debriefing structure to avoid slipping into a treatment modality. Obviously there is limited information on experiences with individual debriefing to offer additional information. Debriefing is historically a group process and therefore its specific strategies and stages are better known than that of debriefing as an individual model.

How long after an incident can debriefing be initiated? When is the best time to debrief?

Debriefing can be initiated between 36 to 72 hours. This, however, is not always possible given the environmental and organizational issues at hand. In disaster situations it may be up to five days, even weeks, before debriefing groups are held simply because environmental issues, rescue efforts, finding shelter, etc. remain the priority.

Yule (1993) suggests that debriefing with children and adolescents is best done between 7-14 days following an incident. I would concur that this is the best time. The immediate needs are to obtain factual information, to restore some sense of order and safety and attempt to meet the first level responses of all involved.

There is no data available supporting the optimal time to initiate the debriefing process. There are benefits to immediate, as well as delayed debriefing. In fact, in my experience, debriefings can actually be conducted months, even years following critical incidents. It is quite common that years later people will immediately return emotionally even physically to their experience as if it happened only a day earlier. This is also seen in professionals who were not debriefed after their involvement in responding to critical incidents as well as surviving victims left unattended.

There are several advantages to waiting a few days before initiating debriefing. First, it is easier to evaluate the overall reaction and stability of all involved. Second, it is easier to gather factual information. Third, it allows individuals the opportunity to rely on their own coping skills to better determine for themselves the need to be involved in debriefing. The same could be said for a school setting where hysterical contagion can make it difficult to determine who needs what services in the first few days.

How long does a debriefing session take?

Using the Mitchell model, debriefing can take as long as three hours. This time frame may prove difficult for school and at agency settings. Johnson (1993) suggests different durations for different developmental levels - preschool-K @ 15-30 minutes; lower elementary @ 30 minutes-1 hour; upper elementary @ 30 minutes-1 hour; junior high @ 45 minutes-1 1/2 hours; and high school @ 1-2 hours.

However, it is important to note that the formal debriefing process is far too cognitive and structured for the preschool and lower elementary levels. This age level will respond more favorable to defusing activities along with some cognitive processing which makes for a longer session and possibly calls for two sessions. **A detailed discussion of defusing can be found in Chapter Eight.**

It may be difficult to retain high school students, as well as staff beyond two hours for debriefing. One wonders how much more can be processed and accomplished after two hours of intense sharing. Clinical experience tells us that after two hours of intense focus the mind and body begin to wander and seek distance from such intensity.

If a debriefing session lasts beyond two hours it may be a signal that 1) there were too many people in the group; 2) a dominant participant was not managed appropriately; 3) the structure of the process was not properly followed. The caution about debriefing going beyond two hours is that it leaves too much room for emotions to become unraveled, for individuals to reveal far more than they intended, for debriefers to fall into role of therapists rather than facilitators and educators.

Our recommendation is that it is always better to return for a second session than to prolong the initial session. Remember, part of the message debriefers want to convey to participants is that as difficult as this has been they are still capable of coping even when there may be additional issues that need to be taken up at an additional session.

How many people can be debriefed at one time?

There is a good deal of disagreement in this area. Johnson (1993) suggests that entire classrooms can be debriefed. Petersen and Straub (1992) recommend a limit of 15-20 participants. Meichenbaum (1994), in his review of debriefing history and models suggest that 6-15 is the maximum.

The basic premise of debriefing is that each participant should have the opportunity to share the details of his experience -- what he saw and heard; his first thoughts; what surprised him about his reactions; all the physical and emotional reactions; etc. This is done in stages by each person. For each of the 8-10 participants to answer all the questions will take approximately two hours. It is virtually impossible to debrief a group of 10 or more people and give each of them adequate time to share the details of his experience. Debriefing is not designed for larger groups. Working with larger groups demands different approaches. (See our discussion on classroom presentations, operational debriefing and defusing.)

Debriefing is reserved for the most-exposed. If there are more than 8-10 most-exposed victims then initiate additional debriefing groups.

Should administrators or other officials be included with line staff?

No. It is best to debrief administrators and other officials separately. The issues are different. The relationships between line staff and administrators can be complex. All of this may inhibit self-disclosure by the staff.

In school settings, however, it is not unusual to find administrators and line staff very supportive of one another. This is understandable since they have the welfare of the children as a focal point. They need to know that each participant will be treated equally and that the debriefing process is not about blame or responsibility. If the debriefers believe that the differences in position will not be a barrier to the process, then proceed. With these things in mind, successful debriefing can be accomplished with a mix of administrators and staff.

School environments are different than agency, organization and community environments. In agency and other settings it is advisable to group people by their position and/or role in the experience, for example witnesses, rescuers, administrators/supervisors, line staff, etc.

Can you have more than one session with the same people in one day?

Yes. As stated earlier it is our belief that two hours is the optimal range of effectiveness to meet. At the same time, participants may need additional time. A morning meeting followed by an evening meeting would be appropriate. A one to two hour break may be sufficient when two hours simply is not enough time to complete the process.

The goal is to stabilize individuals as quickly as possible. Individuals are seen as often as necessary in the first several days.

Can the same people be debriefed over an extended period of time?

Yes. Pynoos and others have returned to the setting as long as one year later to conduct debriefings. Community disasters, for example, deal with numerous external factors that can prolong recovery. Frequently there are ongoing reminders of the trauma. The type of disaster, extent of injuries, deaths, and the potential for reoccurrence can all have prolonged impact on survivors which necessitate further debriefing.

In school systems that have been exposed to multiple deaths over a period of months, one would anticipate the need to return for debriefing after each incident and again a month or two following the last incident. Pennebaker and Harber (1993) who studied peoples reactions after the Loma Prieta earthquake in California saw reactions to the incident change over different periods of time and stated "... just when a trauma becomes old news is when a second wave of adverse affects begin to crest."

It is important to understand the needs of survivors to distance themselves from the terror of their experience. Avoidance brings rest and renewed energy. Ironically once we begin to feel safe, any residual reactions not addressed or relieved initially, will emerge once again.

If a return debriefing is offered, what is the optimum time needed to conduct this additional process?

It will vary from 1/2 hour - 2 hours depending upon the number of participants who return.

Would the same process be used in a follow-up or additional sessions?

Yes, the same process is used. If this were a same day return, individuals may wish to return to a specific issue addressed in the earlier meeting. Each participant should be given the opportunity to share his thoughts and personal reactions to an issue.

If this is a continuation of an incomplete session, a brief review should be given before starting at the point where the process ended. If there is considerable time between sessions, from several weeks to a year, begin with a brief summary of the first meeting, ask if there are any questions and begin at the first stage by asking - "Are there any new or additional memories you have of what you saw, heard, etc. when this first happened or when you first found out?"

Can debriefing be provided to participants (professionals) who have been exposed to different traumas at different times?

Yes. Regardless of the type of incident there are many shared common reactions to traumatic incidents whether violent or non-violent. The terror, fear, worry, hurt, guilt, anger are all quite common. Trauma-specific reactions such as intrusiveness, thoughts, startle reactions, and physical symptoms are shared by most trauma victims.

Actually the debriefing process is an excellent model to use with professionals with varied experiences who might not otherwise receive debriefing on an individual basis. It helps to build a strong supportive network among professionals who realize the commonality of their experiences.

This "mixed" format is not common, yet when used with professionals with varied experiences becomes a valuable learning experience for them as to the need to engage in regular debriefing sessions. Only skilled debriefers with clinical experience should conduct this process.

Chapter Three
How and What Do We Do?

How many debriefers are needed?

Three debriefers are needed for groups of 8-10 participants. The first debriefer usually covers the introductory and fact finding stages, the second covers the personal reaction stages and the third covers the summary stage.

Debriefing can be done with two debriefers. However, if one of the participants should leave, a debriefer needs to accompany that person. This leaves only one person to debrief, a situation which should be avoided. The intensity of the material covered and the need to control the group process are best suited to at least two debriefers. We, therefore, recommend three debriefers in formal debriefing of most-exposed (see pages d and e).

Who can be a debriefer?

Debriefers certainly need to be trained in the differences between grief and trauma for adults and children. They need to have some clinical experience in assessment, and some group experience because of the format. With the use of three debriefers however, one person can be new to the process, do well, and learn quickly with the support and feedback of the other two debriefers.

Some of the reasons schools and agencies have had difficulty in the past with debriefing experiences are that the debriefers were 1) trained in the "Mitchell Model" and unable to adapt this model to the school/agency setting 2) of a different profession and found it difficult to relate to educators and mental health workers or 3) not experienced working with children, adolescents and varied clinical populations age and developmental differences.

Many school districts have moved to District Crisis Teams or Trauma Response Teams and use team members as debriefers. More mental health, child-family agencies and organizations are sending staff for debriefing training, to be better able to assist neighboring schools, staff within their own systems, and other community residents and businesses exposed to traumatic incidents.

Are there times or factors that might indicate a debriefer not debrief?

Yes. Vicarious traumatization is something all debriefers and trauma specialists must continually evaluate. Debriefing is difficult work and exposes debriefers and intervenors to the very reactions they attempt to help others overcome. The constant reexperiencing, intrusive thoughts, images, problems concentrating, staying focused, fatigue, problems controlling feelings, wishing you weren't a team member or responsible for debriefing are all indicators that you need to distance yourself until you can "reclaim" yourself. **It is not advisable to be a debriefer in a situation in which you are familiar with the victim**, such as a therapist, counselor, school administrator, etc. You may think you can manage, but once in the group find that it is too difficult to separate from your own feelings.

In addition, specific situations (incidents) may trigger strong emotional reactions that should preclude debriefing. These reactions will be experienced as you learn of the nature of the incident. This is why it is important to obtain incident information prior to initiating a session. When personal reactions are strong, it might be best to step back and let someone else conduct the debriefing.

At other times you simply may have just come out of a difficult situation and need a rest. Rather than be a direct debriefer, you may be more helpful taking on the role of operational (administrative) debriefer for the debriefing teams (see Chapter Nine).

Are there ground rules?

Most definitely. Debriefing needs to be a very structured process. There is no way to know the emotional stability and well being of participants. Structure encourages the gradual release of those emotions which may otherwise become volatile or out of control. Turnbull (in Meichenbaum, 1994) wrote of his experiences debriefing relief workers following the Lockerbie air disaster:

"We also rapidly learned a cardinal rule in debriefing - **that it is not advisable** to begin with inquiring about the emotional reactions of 'exposure hardened' individuals. It was more effective (and easier) to collect together the overall experience of the group before exploring individual reactions."

Another reason debriefing needs to be a very structured process is because when in crisis, one needs structure and direction for stabilization - for slowing down the adrenaline, the out-of-control sense of powerlessness. Ground rules specific to the process provide this structure and direction.

Ground rules include: (complete detailing of rules and stages can be found in the Appendix)

- Only one person talks at a time
- If you cannot answer the question asked, you may pass and be returned to once others have responded
- There is no blaming, accusing
- There are to be no interruptions - phones and beepers are to be turned off
- Confidentiality is to be maintained, etc.

What about confidentiality?

Participants must be able to trust that their responses will be kept confidential. Often, during such intense sharing, participants may say more than they initially intended, or hear things that are unexpected, even shocking.

Critical Incident Stress Debriefing (CISD) is often used in response to incidents which involve law enforcement, investigators and those participants in the process of being questioned. This generates concern for confidentiality. As a result it is recommended that notes not be taken.

A school-agency situation is likely to be much different and not involve participants who are involved with investigators. Note taking in this case can be reserved for the debriefer who will be completing the summary process. If notes will be taken to aid recall for the summary, it is important to inform participants prior to starting and ask if doing so creates a problem. (See Appendix for recommended statement.)

What do we do with those participants who have been told by police not to talk about details because of ongoing investigation?

They may pass on questions concerning details but can certainly respond to the majority of the questions posed by the different stages. The process can still be very beneficial.

Should law enforcement representatives provide factual information to the group prior to starting the debriefing in cases where such details are available?

No. The value of the process is that each response helps to gradually develop the story, fill in details, correct misperceptions, and reveal new information. The process allows participants to listen to each other, integrate what they hear from one another into their own experience and reactions, and to come to the realization that what they share in common is not necessarily details, but reactions themselves.

If participants have a need to have someone in authority provide factual information, do so by obtaining that information as a debriefer and then integrate it into the summary phase. Do not attempt to introduce factual information in the initial factual stage. This will change the focus of debriefing from being participant generated to debriefer generated. It will block participant's need to tell their story, which is critical to healing. Correcting false information and distorted perceptions is certainly critical but can be accomplished in the summary stage.

Can debriefers be subpoenaed to testify about the information obtained during debriefing?

Yes. Just as anyone can be sued appropriately or inappropriately, anyone can be subpoenaed.

There is no need to keep records or notes of debriefing sessions. Without records it will be difficult to recall "who said what" much less "what" was said. Debriefing is so intense and covers so much that it will be very difficult to recall specifics. This is likely not to be an issue working with schools and agencies, but if it does occur, it is best to consult with an attorney.

When debriefing children, what additional concerns about confidentiality exist?

Children will talk. Maintaining confidentiality may be difficult. It probably is best to say to children something such as: "It is okay to talk to your friends and others about what it was like for you, but it is not okay to tell your friends or others what the others talked about."

What do we say to participants (adults) about phone calls, beepers, attending to students or other clients?

The rule is that phones and pagers are turned off during the session. Participants are not to be available to other staff or clients during debriefing. Interruptions are very detrimental to the value of the process and disruptive to other participants. The purpose of debriefing is to allow participants the time and attention needed to debrief. Being on call and accessible by phone, etc., prohibits this from being accomplished.

How should the room be set up?

Assuming that you accept the recommendations not to have more than 8-10 participants, the space needs to allow for all of you to sit in a circle or around a table. Sometimes a table acts as a "safe support." This is not a sensitivity group. The only purpose for sitting in a circle is for each member to be better able to listen to one another. It is best to have debriefers sit among participants in a gesture of support. When Defusing younger children the space needed will depend upon the activities chosen.

What props, refreshments do we need?

Kleenex is a must. With adults, coffee, pop, water, tea is okay. Once the group starts most will not be drinking. Beverages do sometimes act as a support - a comfort until the process begins. In some cases participants will have lunch or a snack. They may have been on the "front line" all day. Again, this is not psychotherapy. In trauma we need first to feel safe and protected before we can adequately face the experience. Let them eat or drink as they need unless it becomes very disruptive.

Children: Refreshments are not a good idea to have for children until after the session is completed. Children need as few distractions as possible during debriefing. It will be difficult enough for them to stay focused without adding refreshments. The activities in *Helping Children Feel Safe* require very few materials.

What kind of handout material should be made available and when?

Handout materials are needed for adults. They can be provided prior to starting the session or presented following the session. Sometimes providing handouts just before people are getting settled gives participants something concrete to "hold onto" until the sessions begins. Handouts should provide information about 1) the nature of trauma and its reactions 2) ways to take care of oneself when under stress, 3) what signs might indicate a need for additional assistance beyond debriefing, and 4) where to call for additional assistance if needed. (See Appendix)

What procedure needs to be in place prior to debriefing to appropriately begin and end the session?

A supervisor/administrator must be identified and available on premise at all times for two reasons,

1) Occasionally a participant (staff person) will find telling the story or listening to it emotionally overwhelming and will get up and leave. One of the debriefers will need to follow and provide crisis intervention as needed. The supervisor/administrator is legally liable for the participant (staff person). If this person chooses not to return to the group, the supervisor/administrator must make the final decision about allowing the person to leave the premises.

2) During the summary stage you will be asking participants what might be helpful for them during the next several days to best get through those days. Often in schools and agencies, participants will want time off, coverage for clients, etc. These will be requests only administrators can answer. It is appropriate to have a brief discussion with the administrator and ask him to meet with the group, to offer whatever resources or support possible. This can be done before the group ends. Although some decisions may not be immediately possible, just knowing that their requests will be considered and some response will be forthcoming, can relieve some of their stress.

It is wise, as a debriefer, to inform the administrator prior to debriefing that staff may ask for some release time, additional help, or temporary change in duties.

Chapter Four
Debriefing Stages and Process

<u>NOTE</u>: The complete debriefing process, its stages, questions and comments to participants can be found in the Appendix for easy use. In this chapter we will provide a brief review of the stages, their purpose, and issues related to conducting the process.

TLC's experience with schools and agencies has led to a three stage Trauma Debriefing Model: the Introductory Story Stage which includes orientation to the process, sharing of details of each participant's experience and cognitive reactions; the Personal Reaction Stage which includes physical and emotional reactions; and the Summary Stage which includes a review of reactions, normalization, education and preparation, requests from participants for supportive resources and closure.

Do debriefers have a script?

Yes. It is appropriate for each debriefer to have 5 x 7 index cards or a similar format that includes the questions of the assigned stage. It is appropriate to let participants know that you do have a list of the questions you will be asking to help keep you, the debriefer, focused on the process while also listening to the grief and horror of their experiences. It is very easy to become so involved that questions and comments committed to memory may be lost. The notes ensure that all the issues will be covered and that the debriefing process will be comprehensive and as beneficial as possible.

Can debriefers use their own words when asking the debriefing questions?

It is recommended that debriefers follow the script. The questions use specific words and phrases which direct themselves to specific trauma references.

Experience teaches us that when given the flexibility to use ones own words, the focus is often lost, the value of externalizing specific trauma references is minimized, and debriefers tend to become less focused and slip into more traditional clinical interview processes.

Must debriefers always direct questions to participants in the same order?

Remember that a crisis brings terror and fear. Order and structure help reduce that fear and bring about stabilization. By moving around the circle of participants in the same order following each question, participants are given the opportunity to prepare their answer as well as listen to the answers being given as they know when their turn is coming and that the question will be repeated should they not be able to remember the question because of the intrusiveness of thoughts and images being experienced. There is safety and control in the process - the very two experiences victims of trauma struggle to reclaim.

What happens if a debriefer neglects to ask one of the questions assigned to that stage?

Wait until the debriefer has completed the stage. Either debriefer may then ask the missed question before starting the next stage.

Is it appropriate to ask multiple questions of participants at one time?

No. Again, in the state of crisis, simplicity and clarity is essential. These questions are designed to bring focus to specific trauma reactions. Multiple questions not only become confusing, but break down the structured process of asking one question of each participant, one at a time.

Trained counselors, social workers, and psychologists, when first learning how to debrief fall into old patterns of pursuing an issue with multiple questions. Debriefing is not therapy. The debriefing process is quite a different process than most have been trained to use.

When is it appropriate to ask for clarification, to reflect, to normalize?

This question again reflects the methodology so many professionals have been trained to use in individual and group interventions. Yes, there are times to normalize and reflect. However, experience has taught us that when done too early or too frequently it inhibits participants from telling their story.

This issue is similar to a child who is crying as he relates his painful experience. The "gut" reaction may be to give the youngster a hug to comfort him but in fact it would remove him from the pain he so desperately needs to face and externalize. Hugging, whether physically or verbally during the expressing of one's pain shuts down the process at a point where if it is important to "get it out" where it can more easily be resolved or controlled. Too much reflecting, normalizing too early creates the same result.

Reflections, normalizations, even elaboration in our experience can be reserved for the summary stage.

If there are multiple victims involved with the incident being debriefed, how are participants asked about their relationship to and experience with the victims?

This can be managed by asking, "Could you please tell us who you are and to which of the victims you are related? If you are not directly related to the victim, then tell us how you were involved with the incident."

What don't we want to ask initially?

Do not begin by asking participants how they are feeling.

Remember, you may not have any idea how severely participants have been impacted. In a crisis state you want to lower anxiety not increase it. Asking about feelings can quickly and sometimes dangerously escalate reactions to the out of control level. In addition, debriefing is not therapy. It is not the purpose of the process nor your role as debriefer to probe feelings, but to simply identify, acknowledge and later normalize emotional reactions.

What do we ask about initially?

Relationships and facts. By asking participants to explain their relationship to the victim(s) and the details of their exposure to the incident the focus is taken off the emotional intensity they may be experiencing and is placed into the cognitive realm. Sharing concrete information can lesson anxiety and more easily establish a sense of control.

Chapter Five
Responding to Participants

What if someone doesn't want to talk?

No one is required to talk. In fact, one of the initial instructions speaks to this. Any participant who does not wish to answer the question asked may pass by simply indicating such. The debriefer will return to this person once other participants have answered. The participant however, may pass again.

The objective is to create a safe, non-intrusive environment. Some people simply need time to listen and get comfortable enough to become involved. Do not underestimate the power of listening in this process.

It is also important to trust the debriefing process. It is not unusual for someone to remain silent through the first stage. Trust that the trauma questions are designed in such a way as to allow survivors to attach to what is most critical for them to share and that somewhere in the process that will likely happen.

What if a participant does not want to stop talking or continually interrupts?

In the group process a dominant responder frequently emerges. In the debriefing process this often is the person who is having intense emotional reactions to the experience because of the type of relationship to the victim, specific proximity, witnessing of the incident or severe accountability issues.

When initiating the ground rules it is important to stress that only one person talks at a time and in the order established. Indicate that it may be difficult at times because the urge to respond to someone's comment can be very strong. Let them know there will be a place in the process for them to express their personal reactions.

Generally, interruptions occur within the first five-ten minutes of the process if they occur at all. Politely remind the individual of 1) the ground rules, 2) the importance of listening as a part of healing and, 3) that they will have an opportunity to respond when it is their turn.

Usually after the second interruption, this person will be able to stop the interrupting. The reason for this is that as participants around the circle share the details of their experience, all participants become preoccupied with integrating what is being said with their own memories and reactions. In addition, being in a group of peers exerts a good deal of indirect pressure to comply. Any person in such a structured systematic process such as debriefing who cannot control themselves, after the second or perhaps a brief third interruption, may need individual attention. It would be appropriate for one of the debriefers to leave with this person and do some crisis intervention individually.

You will not find a discussion of this type in other sources discussing debriefing because it is delicate. It is rare that you would ever have to ask anyone to leave. You are more likely to have a visibly emotional participant get up and leave because the exposure is too difficult or overwhelming. Leaving for some is a survival behavior. It needs to be permitted, but also evaluated immediately.

What if someone does leave?

It is advisable for one of the three debriefers to follow after and do what is necessary to stabilize the person and ensure his safety. It may also be necessary to transfer responsibility for this person to the available administrator/supervisor.

When only two debriefers remain after a participant leaves, the non-working one needs to prepare himself to assist in the summary work. **Some models suggest not letting participants leave.** Some believe that such behavior is a cry for containment on the part of the individual. This may be the case, but attempts at physical restraint lead to far greater risk and potential liability. **Experience with violent, psychotic populations suggest that, when a client suddenly gets up to bolt out of the office, he is actually exercising self control.** To inhibit or prohibit a person from leaving tends to accelerate the "out of control" reaction and makes an attack or physical assault more probable. **When a participant leaves a debriefing session, trust that he knows what is best for himself, but then follow him out.**

Who is the best debriefer to follow after a participant who leaves?

It should be predetermined that the person doing the summary stage be the person designated to provide emergency intervention should someone leave. The remaining non-working debriefer can pick up the summarizer's tasks. The debriefer assigned to go after a participant needs also to have crisis intervention experience.

Can a person who leaves return to the group?

Yes, if mutually agreed upon by that participant and debriefer.

Who else needs to be involved?

The administrator/supervisor of this individual whom you requested be on premise during the debriefing needs to be immediately, physically "connected up" with the participant should the participant indicate he cannot return to the group.

What liabilities may be in question?

A person who is emotionally upset and directly leaves the premise from the debriefing group could be considered your liability should something happen.

As debriefers you are not placing yourself in the role of therapist. However, you are providing an intervention that puts you in a responsible position for that individual's state of mind. This is why it is so important to leave the decision of the status of that participant in the hands of the responsible administrator/supervisor.

If someone on the team has crisis intervention experience, allow that person to assess the stability of the person and make recommendations for immediate intervention.

Again, it is very unlikely that such extreme measures will ever be needed, but it is a responsibility of yours to be prepared for such contingencies as a debriefer. This is also an ethical responsibility as you have temporarily been given responsibility for the well being of the participants in the group. Professionally you need to be prepared.

What are the remaining participants told should someone get up and leave?

Let them know that you are prepared for this, that it is not unusual, that their colleague will not be left alone. Should the debriefer return without the participant, provide a very brief comment as to the person's status.

What do we do if a participant does not actually answer the question asked?

This is not unusual. Questions are quite specific and concrete to help participants focus, but occasionally the intensity of their reactions will limit their ability to focus. If the specific question is not answered, let the participant finish his answer and then say "Let me repeat the question one more time. What I specifically want you to focus on is..."

Example
Question: What was the first thought you had when this first happened?

Answer: I felt really bad, sick to my stomach, my head was spinning.

Response: Those are all normal feelings, but as you think about it now, what was the first <u>thought</u> you had when this first happened?

What if several answers are given to one question?

When the participant is finished, it may be necessary to restate the question. Let's use the example of the question, "What was your first thought when this first happened or when you first found out?" The participant's response might be multiple for example, "I thought I was going to die and I thought about _____ and if they were okay. I thought about how I was going to make it through this."

Since these are multiple answers and you cannot be sure what the first thought actually was at the time, restate the question. "Let me ask, of all those thoughts you mentioned, what was the first thought you had?"

How do we handle blame and anger?

Blame and anger are reactions that generally surface in the first stage before participants have had the opportunity to listen to one another's stories and reactions.

Should a participant "point the finger" or want to talk about how angry he is with what happened, or with someone or something related to the incident, respond in the following way:

(Blame) "Please let me remind you that we are not here to accuse or "point the finger." This is not about right or wrong but about telling your stories and realizing that much of all you are experiencing is not unusual. You will find as we go along that probably you share many of the same reactions."

(Anger) "Anger is a very natural reaction to the kind of traumatic experience you have been exposed to. There will be an opportunity for you to talk about these feelings later when we are dealing with your personal reactions. For now what we would like you to focus on is..."

CAUTION: Anger is a normal part of the grieving process and an expected reaction to some parts of the trauma experience. However, it is one of those emotions that can quickly escalate. As a debriefer you must be constantly alert to the possibility that anger can become explosive. **Given the fact that you usually do not know the participants, you do not want to allow anyone to actually become expressively angry.**

It is permissible in the debriefing process for a participant to say, "It makes me mad to think about the life that has been taken" or "It makes me angry to think about all the hurt people that are suffering because of what _____ did (or happened)."

As a debriefer you do not want to allow a participant to go beyond identifying the anger that has been created. The purpose of debriefing is to stabilize reactions of the individuals, not to encourage a complete catharsis of emotion. It is not meant to be a sensitivity group or a psychotherapy session. Even in psychotherapy, anger is an emotion that is approached slowly, over time.

Along with being a precursor to violence, anger can also be viewed as a cover for more intense reactions of fear, guilt, shame, powerlessness, or vulnerability. Allowing the cover to come off too quickly can overwhelm an individual and leave him far more vulnerable and fragile.

What do we do when participants bring up policy, procedures, staffing, administrative or management issues specific to the incident?

The primary purpose of an initial debriefing session is not to problem solve, but to acknowledge existing problems related to the incident and its victims/survivors. If issues arise, then communicate the group's concerns to the administrators in the positions to respond. If problem solving does occur, it will be focused on the ways individuals can take care of themselves while recovering from their traumatic experience.

Focusing on administrative, procedural issues, etc., may indeed be a legitimate concern and may need to be addressed immediately, but not during the initial stages of the debriefing process. It is okay to allow a participant to mention a concern but not discuss it. The best way to manage participants who want to focus on such issues is to respond in the following way: "These may be very legitimate concerns and even demand immediate attention. You will have an opportunity later in the process to address these issues, but at this point in time we really need to focus on ... "

Bringing up such issues can be similar to blaming and accusing and attempting to unload one's anger. It can be a way of avoiding the more intense and difficult reactions created by the trauma.

In the Summary Stage participants will in fact be asked what they need to help them better move through the next several days. Generally, they will make suggestions that will need supervisory or administrative approval such as time off.

In the debriefing model such suggestions are taken immediately to the responsible party who has already been informed that their presence in the facility during debriefing is required. With participant consensus you will present the suggestions immediately and have that responsible person meet with them once the debriefing is finished. In our experience, most of the suggestions made allow for easy approval by the administrator, unless they involve more complicated issues in the system.

What do we do when participants begin to get up and comfort one another with hugs?

Allow briefly, then suggest "when reactions are as intense as they are following a traumatic experience, we need the opportunity to get them out in all their detail, to get them outside ourselves so others can be a witness to them, and so we can better control them. Comforting (hugging) too early in the process can actually prohibit and stop this process. We know by the end of the session there will be tremendous support and you will feel comforted. So, for right now, let's see if we can continue to hear all the details. It will be easier to deal with these once they are out in front of you."

Quickness to comfort can frequently be a way to shut down a persons reactions, not because that person is necessarily finding it too painful to share, but because they trigger fear in the person rushing to comfort. One of the positive benefits of debriefing is that participants learn that once they are able to tell their story they do actually feel more in control, as well as feel relief from the fears associated with their reactions.

In the Summary Stage is it essential to reference the responses heard from each participant?

It is important to identify specific reactions and to normalize them but it is not critical that you remember who described which reactions.

How do you initiate a discussion about the positive factors that have emerged from other experiences?

Simply ask - "As tragic as this is, as you look at all the people it has impacted, what is the most positive aspect that has emerged for you?"

Often participants will talk about the support they received and how strong their clients and students have been throughout the entire ordeal. This becomes an excellent way to end the debriefing session.

Chapter Six
At Risk

What are the issues related to potentially at risk participants?

All survivors of a trauma-inducing incident are potentially at risk for chronic stress or posttraumatic stress. It is difficult to determine who may be at risk during that initial four week acute stress period due to delayed reactions and all the factors in the environment which prolong and or induce delayed reactions. It is therefore recommended that following an initial debriefing period, a second session be scheduled sometime after the four week period. The purpose of this session is to better identify those survivors who are not coping well and may indeed be experiencing more severe reactions and symptomology.

Assessment for potentially at risk individuals is complex. In disaster situations assessment is compounded by environmental factors, community response and resources available. Law enforcement, the judicial system, the media can all contribute to such factors for survivors. Solomon & Green (1992) propose that vulnerability to more severe reactions can be identified during three different periods: 0-to-3 months, 3-to-18 months and 18 months plus.

Meichenbaum (1994) reviews numerous assessment tools and criteria of vulnerability. He identifies 58 items and classifies them under three headings: 1) Characteristics of the Disaster; 2) Characteristics of the Post Disaster; 3) Responses and Characteristics of the Individual and Group.

Most often schools and agencies request debriefing following incidents not directly threatening the lives of the entire community such as, suicide, overturned school bus, sudden death of student or staff person, shootings, or car fatalities. Occasionally debriefing is requested following community disasters such as floods, hurricanes, or terrorism.

Although disasters generate more potential for at risk survivors than non--catastrophic incidents, each share common factors. Some factors placing survivors at risk are: proximity to the incident, the duration, exposure to grotesque death or critical injury, perception of a threat to life, the experience of powerlessness, somatic reactions, lack of support, exposure to continued stress, secondary victimization, and prior exposure to a traumatic incident. Exposure to these factors may necessitate additional follow up beyond the first four weeks.

Participants in the Summary Stage of debriefing need to be told the following - Should the reactions you are experiencing now during the first four weeks continue anytime after the four week period it will be in your best interest to call us (or contact a trauma specialist). Again, it will not be unusual for these reactions to continue or emerge later. It takes time to recover from a trauma. The real concern is that if you do not get some assistance, these reactions may not only become chronic but trigger additional problems for you. Do not hesitate to call TLC (or contact a trauma specialist).

It is beneficial for staff from school and agency settings to be debriefed by trained debriefers from neighboring agencies versus debriefing by their own staff. It provides participants with a contact person they can call directly and in confidence should additional assistance be needed.

It is also beneficial to follow the initial debriefing with a follow up session anytime after the initial four weeks - for example, at three months, nine months, to one year (Williams et al. 1994) as a precaution against chronic reactions not previously addressed.

There are several diagnostic tools available for identification of reactions and their level of severity. Although not typically used in the initial debriefing session, having a baseline and follow up assessment comparing participants initial reactions with reactions at three months or one year can be very helpful.

What assessment tools exists to evaluate for PTSD and level of severity?

The TLC Institute has available a child/adolescent diagnostic PTSD Survey for children 6-18 years of age. This assessment tool identifies the specific trauma reactions present, the DSM-IV subcategory they fall under and their level of severity.

If a participant needs individual attention, what do we do?

Should a participant lose control and exhibit behaviors which are of concern but not life threatening, it is appropriate for a debriefer to recommend additional help to that individual before leaving him with the responsible administrator.

If the concern is for that individual's safety because of potential suicidal behavior, then the liability and choices are quite clear - you must inform the administrative supervisor of your concern preferably in the presence of the potentially suicidal individual and the responsible administrator. The school or agency's protocol for responding to potentially suicidal students or staff are then to be instituted by the administrative supervisor. You are responsible for making sure this happens. Failure to follow through on your part could be viewed as negligence. We recommend *Trauma Response Protocol Manual For Schools* (Steele,W., et. al., 2000) for schools who do not have a protocol in place.

Additionally, should there be concern for a participant's ability to drive home, return to operating vehicles or machines which could place that person or others at risk, you would also inform the administrator/supervisor to determine the most appropriate intervention.

Because debriefing is so structured and generally occurs three or more days after the incident, these concerns generally do not arise. Nevertheless, as a debriefer it is your responsibility to be prepared and to act responsibly.

Who is ultimately responsible for that person's safety?

There is no reason for one individual to carry the burden of determining what is best for an at-risk individual. This is the joint responsibility of the debriefers, administrators/supervisors and crisis teams.

As a debriefer, you are acting in the role of facilitator - not a clinician or intervention specialist. You are providing assistance, support and the opportunity for participants to talk about their experiences. Should concern for a participant arise, your role is to provide additional support and assistance by informing the responsible administrator. You may also need to do some immediate crisis intervention. **Never** by yourself, however, make the final determination of what is best for the individual. Consult with the other debriefers and the administrator/supervisor.

Are there characteristics which distinguish victims from survivors?

Yes. Victims believe they are powerless to take control of their life - that bad things have to be accepted because there is nothing that can be done about them. Victims do not feel they deserve to be loved because they are flawed, inept, inadequate. Victims usually have little energy and often isolate themselves because they believe no one can be trusted and no one could possibly understand the ordeals they have experienced.

Survivors become survivors as they take a direct active role in healing. They realize choices are always available and that despite their experiences they can always learn, improve, and create a better future with personal meaning. They realize there will be disappointments but that these too are manageable. They see themselves as deserving of love and support.

The major difference between victims and survivors is that survivors can reach out and accept help, whereas victims passively wait for help to come their way but when available cannot embrace it.

In Appendix C there is a comparative list of victim/survivor statements. Such statements are excellent assessment indicators.

When do we make a referral for additional assistance?

Your ability to recognize a participant's need for additional assistance will be partly based upon intervention experiences with traumatized individuals and your understanding of "the risk to self or others" they pose.

It is imperative that you not only know the differences between grief and trauma but are able to recognize these through behavior, verbalization and responses to trauma-specific questions.

The debriefing process asks very trauma-specific questions. These questions are designed to provide information needed to build a picture of the kinds of stress reactions each participant is experiencing. The key issues become 1) can the individual function with some level of normalcy and 2) do they have an available support system? Realizing that you may initially be debriefing individuals during the acute stress stage, and that these reactions may not go beyond this period, **you need to check back in several weeks to best determine the person's status at that time.**

If a participant has a limited support system (one that is not willing to learn about trauma, listen to the victim, nor encourage the telling of their story, etc.) this person is likely to find recovery more difficult and needs to be encouraged after the initial debriefing to have a follow up visit.

The individual who is having difficulty returning to their level of functioning prior to the trauma four weeks beyond the acute stress stage, is going to need additional intervention. Forgetting that one has something boiling on the stove, coming in late to work, unable to perform at a level prior to the trauma, difficulty concentrating, difficulty completing tasks are all indicators that additional assistance is needed when continuing beyond that four week period.

But what about those situations in which the school, agency, or individuals themselves do not follow through with an additional session? All you have are the observations and information of that first session.

Certainly anyone talking about suicide requires immediate referral. Anyone talking about previous trauma that the current situation has exacerbated needs help. Statements like, "I'm not sure I can handle or get over this," "I'm not able to sleep," "My mind just can't focus," are not unusual, yet indicate that a referral should be considered if these reactions persist.

Chapter Seven
Debriefer Concerns

Can we debrief ourselves?

Yes, but not as effectively as having another trained debriefer take you through the process. **Occasionally, you will not have access to others.** When that occurs we recommend using the Abbreviated Debriefers Debriefing format found in Appendix E.

Can already existing crisis team members act as debriefers for their own staff?

Yes, but here, too, some objectivity will be lost and there may be confidentiality issues between participants which prohibit an "open" debriefing.

We recommend the use of trained debriefers from an area agency or private practice.

What happens if one of us becomes upset during the debriefing process?

Although there will be times when your heart is touched and torn, when details begin to physically sicken you or frighten you, you are expected to be able to remind yourself that this is not about you and return your focus to taking care of the victims. Obviously this is why it is so important to be debriefed yourself. We'll discuss vicarious traumatization shortly.

As a debriefer, it is your responsibility to learn what you can about the incident before hand. If what you learn triggers negative reactions, creates anxiety, and leaves you wondering whether you will be able to cope with the details, then you need to say "no" to debriefing that incident.

If you are new to debriefing then it is best to take on the Summary Stage while letting the two most experienced debriefers handle the first two stages. It is sometimes easier to manage surprising and unpleasant personal reactions when you know you have time to collect yourself before starting your assigned stage.

Generally, training and working initially with experienced debriefers will prevent a situation where a debriefer actually becomes a participant. Know your debriefers. We do not recommend debriefing with someone you have not worked with or trained with previously to minimize the chance of such a situation happening.

If a debriefer should lose control, attempt to normalize the situation by saying, "Listening to your story and details is difficult for us as well. Sometimes they trigger memories of our own personal reactions and do it at a time when we least expect."

This may give the debriefer time to regain control. If not, debriefers need to be prepared to assume that debriefer's role. It might be best for that debriefer to excuse himself even though this is not the best role modeling for the rest of the participants.

The likelihood that this would happen is quite rare. Good training, preparation prior to entering the process, and working with those you know should prevent such a situation.

Are there special issues to address when debriefing the debriefers?

Debriefers need to undergo the same debriefing process they have used with the participants. The questions are somewhat different in order to address processing issues. **We recommend the Debriefers Debriefing format found in the Appendix.**

What are the transference and countertransference issues debriefers must evaluate?

Transference refers to the relationship a victim transfers to the helper. At the core of trauma is utter terror and powerlessness. It is similar to the kind of dream where we are in severe danger, try to scream for help, but nothing comes out. With this in mind it is easier to understand that, "The greater the patient's (participants) emotional conviction of helplessness and abandonment the more desperately the need for an omnipotent rescuer (Herman, 1992). In such a state individuals will expect much from the interviewer, as a rescuer.

Countertransference refers to the helper's reaction to being a witness to trauma through the retelling of its details by the victim. The same victim's response of being overwhelmed emotionally can be experienced by the interviewer simply by listening to the details (Saigh,1991). Even experienced interviewers can come to feel unskilled in the midst of all the terror, horror, and helplessness being expressed by victims when telling their story.

In debriefing, countertransference always needs to be a concern of debriefers. The cumulative impact of being witness to the experiences of multiple victims can trigger anger, helplessness, fear, and even "witness guilt" (Herman, 1992). The experience can become so intense that debriefers may become depressed or judge themselves negatively for not being compassionate enough. They may feel guilty for wanting to limit the time spent as a debriefer, or for causing the victims intense pain by encouraging them to retell and return to the experience.

Strong indicators of "debriefing burnout" include: assuming too much responsibility for victim's lives; taking on additional or excessive responsibility; shying away from exploring victim's experiences, when it is appropriate to do so; experiencing depersonalizing or dissociative reactions.

Because debriefing is not therapy and is limited by the number of sessions, transference is not likely to become a significant issue for debriefers. Countertransference on the other hand, is very real because of the multiple exposure in even one session.

To avoid the cumulative impact of such exposure and vicarious traumatization, which can and does occur, it becomes essential that debriefers go through periodic debriefing.

What shouldn't debriefers do immediately following the end of a debriefing session?

What you do not want to do immediately after a debriefing is get into your car to get to that next appointment. Your adrenaline will be producing at a high level in response to your exposure to the details of the trauma. The adrenaline will push that speedometer to an unsafe speed without you realizing it because your brain will be distracted by efforts to process what you heard or to distance yourself from the visualizations and graphic details. In either case your driving concentration will suffer and place you and others at risk.

What you need to do is to take fifteen minutes to walk around, do some deep breathing, and progressive relaxation before putting the key in the ignition.

Debriefing is stressful. Be aware of its potential to induce stress quickly and at times without your awareness. Adopt a preventative attitude and behavior by being debriefed following your exposures and practicing basic stress reduction activities - deep breathing, progressive relaxation, etc.

Is there a format for debriefing debriefers?

Yes. You will find a Debriefing Debriefers model in Appendix E.

Chapter Eight
Classroom Presentations
Classroom Debriefing

Does debriefing work in classrooms?

No. The formal debriefing process, even reduced to the three phase model we recommend for schools and agencies will run a good two hours with eight-to-ten participants. It would be impossible to move adequately through each phase with twenty-five to fifty students.

Debriefing is also a very cognitive process in its original form, far too cognitive for younger children.

Furthermore, debriefing should be reserved for those who are the most-exposed to the incident. Not all members in a classroom would necessarily be classified as the most-exposed.

Others (Johnson, 1993) suggest that an entire classroom can be debriefed. An entire classroom can effectively be assisted following a critical incident, but the use of debriefing as a process for an entire classroom is not recommended.

There is no doubt that individual variations of debriefing are being used in schools and agencies and are being referred to as debriefing. In fact they more often reflect crisis intervention or mix a myriad of processes from supporting emotional catharsis to providing information and education about grief and trauma. This handbook recommends for schools the use of the following:

a) Classroom presentations within the first three days following an incident to minimize unwanted student responses, to educate and normalize grief and trauma reactions, and to inform them of the activities the school will be initiating to assist those in need.

(See Appendix D for a brief outline of a classroom presentation which is taken from *Trauma Response Protocol Manual For Schools* (Steele, W., et. al., 2000), and is recommended for those developing crisis response teams, upgrading teams, or inservicing new team members).

b) Identification of those most-exposed to the trauma and crisis intervention assessment as soon as possible - but always within two days.

c) Debriefing the most-exposed approximately three-to-seven days following the incident in groups of no more than 8 - 10 participants; observation of most-exposed over the following four week period with individual/group intervention provided as needed.

d) Defusing with younger children, following the same guidelines used for debriefing participants.

e) Additional organized responses and activities associated with crisis response teams.

f) A four-to-six week follow-up debriefing of original debriefing groups.

g) The debriefing of crisis team members approximately four-to-five days following the initial organized response assuming that a consultant(s) is available to team members and administrators during the crisis to assist them in their efforts to stabilize students and staff.

h) Administrative (operational) "debriefing" to address critical issues, identify at risk students/staff, student/staff needs, and resources needed to better move through the days ahead. (See Appendix G for Operational Debriefing outline.)

So, can you debrief a classroom? No. Do classroom students need assistance following a critical incident? Yes, but it will vary. Not all will need debriefing but all will need and can benefit from a classroom presentation. This presentation will: provide answers to their questions; normalize their reactions; inform them of upcoming related activities; educate and prepare them for dealing with future reactions and issues that may be triggered in the days ahead.

How is defusing different than debriefing?

Petersen and Straub (1994) define defusing as "the ventilation of thoughts and emotions immediately following a tragic event." They describe this process as one of providing information, promoting ventilation, preparing students and parents for possible reactions, normalization, suggestions for coping, and information as to what will be taking place over the next several days.

Mitchell and Everly (in Meichenbaum 1994) utilize defusing with rescue and treatment specialists during the immediate or protracted aftermath involving rescue and search. Their process includes: the factual exploration of the incident by each of the participants; education about recognizing stress; specific trauma reactions; the need for taking care of oneself physically; teaching coping techniques for dealing with visual and other sensory responses to the exposure.

This description is basically a description of what we consider to be a Classroom Presentation. However, the authors fail to address the issue of the processes to be used with younger children (first to sixth grade) to facilitate the externalization and release of their sensory reactions for which they do not have words.

What are the goals of defusing and appropriate age level of participants?

The goals for defusing are the same as those of debriefing. The only distinctions are the process and age of participants. Age of participants can range from preschool to twelve years. The process involves some cognitive work, but drawing and story telling are also used to help them relate the details of their experience. It is more process oriented than cognitive driven.

Is there anyone who should not be in the defusing process?

Give each child a chance to start the process. However, if a child becomes disruptive by interrupting while others are speaking, interfering with others engaged in psychomotor activities, or damaging another student's work, or simply refuses to participate he should be removed immediately and assisted individually.

Trauma has a way of bringing people together. Structure and a safe environment will help establish control. The defusing model offered in the handbook is structured and helps reduce the fear and worry induced by trauma. However, it still may not be effective for all children. There is no such thing in trauma as resistance. Either a child feels safe to participate or he does not. The focus must always be on safety.

How many can participate at one time in defusing?

An entire class can participate, however, it is recommended that defusing sessions be limited to 8 - 10 children whenever possible. If a larger group is necessary, add another facilitator for every additional 8 - 10 children. Additional time will be needed to give each child the opportunity to display their drawings and tell their stories and for defusers to provide the appropriate reframing, normalization and education.

How long can a defusing session run?

Depending upon age levels and the telling of their stories, fears and worries, sessions can run approximately 30-to-90 minutes.

Keep in mind that part of the process involves psychomotor activities which will take time to complete. These activities will help release and externalize the fear, worry, and anxiety for which they are not likely to have words.

What are the stages of defusing?

(See Appendix G for specific questions, activities) There are <u>five</u> defusing stages in the model:

<u>Introduction</u> - Information related to the incident is shared along with acknowledgement of the different ways they are feeling, what you will be doing to help them, and the ground rules they are to follow.

<u>Generalization</u> - In this phase, before asking about the specific incident itself, the nature of the incident is generalized and the children are asked to share who has had a friend or family member who has experienced a similar type of situation.

For example, a teacher is suddenly killed in an auto accident. Before asking or answering questions about the specific details of the teacher's death, the incident is generalized. The initial focus begins with their understanding of what an accident is and who in their family or someone they know has had an accident, what kind, etc. Examples of reflective summary statements for an accident can include: *Sometimes accidents only hurt people a little. Sometimes a lot. And sometimes people die in accidents (depending upon age level their understanding of death, its permanency, etc., will need to be explored). Sometimes other people cause accidents. Sometimes accidents happen because we are not paying attention, and sometimes accidents just happen and no one is to blame.*

<u>Specification</u> - Once children have had the opportunity to share stories about their knowledge or experiences with the more generalized nature of the incident, they will be ready to move to the specific incident itself.

In this stage very brief details are provided and the children are asked several questions regarding what they have been told or have heard (about their teacher). This is followed by answering any questions they have about what happened to the victim(s).

<u>Externalization</u> - The first three stages could take 10 - 15 minutes to complete. Following the third stage processing takes on the form of psychomotor activities designed to help children externalize their reactions and regain some sense of power over them. Drawing and story telling are used as an impetus for them to make us a witness to the experience as they know it internally but for which they may not have words.

The value and benefits of drawing are well documented. The field-test and research conducted by the TLC Institute of its trauma-specific group and individual intervention strategies, which rely heavily on drawing, validate (Raider and Steele, 2001) what other trauma specialists have also found.

Roje (1995) describes the benefits of drawing for children following the 1994 Los Angeles earthquake. Byers (1996) describes the outcome of drawing and art activities in six mental health clinics in the West Bank and Gaza. Malchiodi (1998) provides an excellent historical view of the art of drawing and devotes an entire chapter to drawing and trauma.

The drawing process accomplishes the following:

- Drawing is a psychomotor activity that allows a person to move from a passive victim stance to an active survivor stance
- It gives a person the opportunity to externalize the traumatic event
- It provides a safe vehicle of communication for a person to tell the details of his story
- Drawing provides a manageable container in which to put the trauma
- It provides a stimulus for storytelling
- It provides a sense of control and empowerment since drawings can be changed, erased or thrown away
- Drawing communicates visually what children do not always have words to describe

In this process children may be asked to draw a picture of the event and tell a story about it. Additional trauma-specific questions will be asked to help them tell their story and externalize their reactions. They will be asked what the worst, hardest, scariest parts were for them. They will be asked what there biggest worry is now and to show how big their worry is at the time.

In this group process children learn that they are not alone with their fears and worries, that others are having or have had the same reactions; that these are not unusual. They will experience some relief from their fear and worry and support from one another. Individually, it will take longer to see results because of the absence of the feedback and support from peers. Group participation is encouraged whenever possible.

Closure - This is the final stage. Cognitive reframing is accomplished via the summary and metaphorical reflections which the children are provided. The major focus is on the meaning of becoming survivors. This is best accomplished through a brief summary, reflective statements (cognitive reframing). NOTE: The defusing process format can be found in the appendix.

Is there a good book to read to younger children while participating in debriefing that speaks directly about trauma and how to feel better?

There is a trauma-specific story which is highly recommended. The book is called *Brave Bart: A Story for Traumatized and Grieving Children (Sheppard, 1998)*, a story of a kitten who is traumatized by a very bad, sad, and scary thing but is helped by Helping Hannah, a neighborhood cat. The story tells how Brave Bart, the traumatized kitty (the victim), becomes Brave Bart, the survivor. *Brave Bart* is available through the TLC Institute.

If we are defusing a group of children following murder, how do we generalize murder?

Murder is violence. Begin with violence. Yesterday _____ was shot and killed - he was murdered. It makes us sad and mad and scared. Before we talk about what happened to _____ , we need to talk about violence.

EXAMPLE: *Violence is when someone hurts someone else really bad, even though they may not die but just get hurt bad. Violence can be when someone gets really mad and yells and screams and we think they might hurt us or someone else. Who can give me an example of something violent they have seen on television, or with someone they know?*

This will be followed briefly by several questions and explanations of how it affects its victims. Following this, you move to the specific incident.

As can be seen, different incidents will dictate somewhat different scripts in the way of explanations and reflections (cognitive reframing) that will be needed. These should be prepared ahead and actually be a part of the trauma response protocol.

What if participants need more assistance after debriefing or defusing sessions; what type of intervention is recommended?

To determine the need, it is likely that you will do so in a follow-up session beyond the four week Acute Stress period discussed earlier. On occasion observations will encourage you to move immediately with additional intervention. Referral to outside sources need to be those with trauma-specific training. TLC does provide several intervention options for use in schools and/or by agency staff trained as trauma consultants. The *"What Color Is Your Hurt?"* program is a ten session trauma-specific group or individual intervention program for pre-school aged children and is designed for use in school settings or agencies. The *"I Feel Better Now!"* program is an ten session, trauma-specific evidence basedgroup program for traumatized children six to ten years old also designed for use in schools or agencies. The *"Trauma Intervention Program"*, short-term intervention model, is an eight session, trauma-specific researched intervention model for use on an individual basis with children six to twelve years old and adolescents up to eighteen years of age. It also is designed for school or agency use.

These programs have all had extensive field-testing and research and have proven invaluable in providing structured, trauma-specific relief for children over a brief period of time. They are designed for use with both violent and non-violent incidents and structured to meet the limitations of school settings regarding intervention, yet address the immediate clinical needs of children being seen in agency settings (see Appendix H for additional information).

Recommended:

For additional defusing activities designed to help create a sense of safety for young children, we recommend *Helping Children Feel Safe*. This booklet provides a variety of sensory activities which give children alternative ways, for use in the classroom and in agency settings, to master their fears and relieve their anxiety.

Chapter Nine
Operational Debriefing

How do we debrief an entire staff?

Previous discussions indicated that debriefing is reserved for the most-exposed and is conducted with 8 - 10 participants in a session. In our view an entire staff cannot be debriefed nor do all staff need debriefing.

Staff, however do need assistance. Rather than fight the national trend of misusing the term, *debriefing*, the process for assisting staff will be referred to as Operational Debriefing (OD). NOTE: The specific series of questions and procedures for OD are located in Appendix G.

What are the goals of an OD session?

The goals of OD sessions are 1) to evaluate the current status of staff and students or clients, 2) to share new information and clarify rumors, 3) to determine the additional needs for immediate resources and support, 4) to prepare staff for possible upcoming problems/reactions, 5) to address taking care of themselves and 6) to reinforce the positive aspects emerging from the crisis.

How much time should be devoted to OD sessions?

It is important to realize that school, mental health, child and family agency staff today are burdened with overwhelming responsibilities to students and clients. Their time is at a premium.

Furthermore, in the midst of a crisis, staff will have put forth a great deal of energy in responding to students or clients as well as one another.

To attempt to conduct an OD session beyond two hours at the end of the work day, is asking a great deal.

It is far better to schedule a one hour session and from that session determine the need for additional sessions. In school situations for example, it is not unusual for crisis teams and staff to spend an entire week providing organized interventions to stabilize the student and staff population. Two-to-three OD after school sessions might be held to monitor the well being of all, to determine needed adjustments and resources for all involved.

Are administrators involved in OD sessions?

This is a judgement call. Over the past eighteen years I have found that, in the midst of a crisis, most line staff and administrators in school settings are very supportive of one another, and in fact, exhibit strong open communication. This is somewhat different than experiences with mental health and other child/family organizations.

Participation of school administrators in OD sessions rarely presents a barrier. Many staff appreciate the opportunity to answer OD questions in the presence of administrators to encourage immediate action. Administrators appreciate it because it generally provides them the opportunity to demonstrate their support.

Participation of administrators/supervisors have in clinical settings, however, created barriers to open communication. The focus of this handbook is such that it is not beneficial to discuss the potential reasons for this dynamic. It is sufficient to say that when conducting OD and debriefing sessions in agencies, the recommendation is to conduct separate sessions with administrative staff.

Are handout materials different for OD sessions than for debriefing sessions?

Handouts detailing the types of reactions to expect following a trauma are similar. Some additional material however, will be needed to address specific needs of staff, students or clients.

It is assumed that handouts related to observation of specific behaviors in students (clients), the need to refer these children and how to do so during the crisis period have been presented at the initial meeting of all staff. These documents, as well as debriefing handouts ought to be already in handout form and in the computer (and hard copies in a crisis response plan) for quick, easy access. There is no need to develop this type of material during the middle of a crisis. *Trauma Response Protocol Manual For Schools* (Steele,W., et. al., 2000) is an excellent resource. (Handouts are also provided in Appendix G.)

What specific questions are asked during an OD session?

There are four OD stages: Stage One: Students/Client Issues; Stage Two: Staff Reactions; Stage Three: Administrator Issues; Stage Four: Summary Stage.

The first set of questions relate to student/client issues. The reason for this is that it is initially far easier to answer questions about students or clients than it is to answer questions about our own behavior. It also helps to put staff in the "motion" of answering questions so when the focus is placed on them, the responses come easier.

The second set of questions relate to their own personal reactions followed by administrative issues.

The third set of questions deal with specific procedural issues and the fourth set of questions are limited to questions they may have of you as debriefers following your summary. Much like debriefing, a summary of the session and their overall response to and reactions from the trauma need to be normalized and some preparation provided for possible near future reactions yet to come.

How many debriefers are needed for an OD session and who should conduct it?

Ideally two debriefers maximize the potential for the best results but because of the structured nature of the process, its purposes and limited duration, one debriefer can manage. **OD should be conducted by an outside trauma specialist** who can remain more objective and address what may be otherwise difficult issues for internal staff to address with their own peers.

What is the purpose for a follow up OD session?

It is important to maintain open communication during a crisis period. It is equally important to keep information flowing at all levels, addressing each distinct population - teachers, transportation staff, etc. Follow-up sessions help to solve problems immediately, identify additional needed resources and prepare for the days to come.

59

Chapter Ten
Training

What kind of training is needed for debriefing in schools and agencies?

Keep in mind that debriefing is just one component of an overall organized crisis response to critical, traumatic incidents.

Trauma reactions are also different from grief reactions and the processes for responding need also be somewhat different than responses to grief. Factors related to risk levels following trauma are also different than those following grief.

A solid foundation of understanding and recognition of these differences followed by appropriate interventions does necessitate training. The Institute requires its Certified Trauma and Loss School Specialists, Specialists, Consultants, and Consultant Supervisors to take a designated number of presentations. See Appendix additional information about TLC and the Certification Program.

Appendix A
A Self Assessment Tool
For
School and Agency
Professionals

William Steele, MSW. PsyD
©1998 TLC Institute
Revised 2003

About this Tool

This self assessment tool will provide you with an awareness of the types of information, training and tools trauma specialists need to help traumatized children find relief from the terror of their experience. It will allow you to compare your status with those school and agency professionals who, after completing the Institute's Certification Program for Trauma and Loss School Specialist, Specialist, or Consultant, score 100%.

The scoring range suggests that you are at a high level of preparedness or are in need of additional information, training, and trauma specific resource materials. This tool is designed for use by educational psychologists, clinical psychologists, pediatric psychologists, marriage and family therapists, licensed professional counselors, school counselors and social workers, school crisis team members, bereavement specialists, pastoral counselors, art therapists, play therapists, nurses, suicidologists, victims assistance specialists, healthcare, hospice, and community mental health professionals.

It is important to understand that a high score may reflect a high level of preparedness but not necessarily a high level of effectiveness as a trauma intervenor. TLC established it's Certification Program to help you determine what a paper questionnaire cannot - your ability to maximize the trauma-specific intervention strategies and programs designed by TLC to help you better help traumatized children find relief from the terror of their experience whether you are working in a school setting or agency setting.

Part 1 · Team Readiness: Instructions

To be completed by all professionals in school or agency settings who are members of the crisis response team. Answer **YES** or **NO** to each question. If you are unsure of an answer, or doubt that a **YES** answer is completely applicable, mark the answer to that question **NO**.

If you answered **NO** to any of the questions, it reflects a weakness in the crisis team's composition and readiness.

About Your Team
DO YOU MEET QUARTERLY?

Score 100% for a YES answer to this question. Anything less than a 100% score reflects a lack of preparedness, which goes beyond simply having protocol in place. Relationships are critical. Knowing one another's area of expertise and comfort are critical. Playing out scenarios, asking "What if...?" identifying roles, responsibilities, and tasks needed for each scenario, are all critical elements to having an effective and efficient team response. Only quarterly meetings can support these tests.

Quarterly meetings and role playing prepares all of the members to respond consistently and cohesively in the middle of chaos, to reach a more immediate resolution of various critical incidents. Without quarterly meetings you are simply a group of people coming together in the middle of a crisis having to find and review protocols. Confidence, competence and leadership that quarterly meetings otherwise build will be lacking as will your effectiveness.

Team - Readiness

YES	NO	
☐	☐	If you are part of a district-wide team, does each school in the district have a minimum of two staff members on the team who have had the same training as the district wide team?
☐	☐	Are critical local resource persons members of your team (community mental health, clergy, law enforcement, PTA/PTO representative, etc.) ?
☐	☐	Are they "mandated" to also attend quarterly meetings to better clarify each of their roles, tasks, etc. when running through various scenarios?
☐	☐	Do you always have immediate access to primary team members?
☐	☐	Can you identify specific resources local community business owners could provide during a crisis as well as what their supportive roles might be?
☐	☐	Are staff home phone numbers and phone tree procedures updated annually?
☐	☐	Has your team/staff rehearsed with your local police an active shooter scenario?
☐	☐	Does each team member have several protocol manuals so they always have immediate access to them?

Part 2 - Member Readiness: Instructions

To be completed by all professionals in school or agency settings who are responsible for responding to potentially traumatized children. Answer **YES** or **NO** to each question. If you are unsure as to whether or not you can accurately answer **YES** to a question, mark that question **NO**.

Can You Identify . . .

YES **NO**

☐ ☐ 5 major differences between grief and trauma?

☐ ☐ At least 8 trauma specific reactions which are different from grief reactions?

☐ ☐ Difference between grief driven dreams and trauma driven dreams?

☐ ☐ The differences between grief driven anger and trauma driven anger?

☐ ☐ At least 10 trauma-specific questions to ask any traumatized child or adolescent?

☐ ☐ The 4 ways a child can become vulnerable to posttraumatic stress disorder (PTSD?)

☐ ☐ The 3 sub-categories in the DSM-IV which contain the trauma-specific reactions which can occur following a traumatic incident?

☐ ☐ The one trauma-specific reaction not found in the DSM-IV?

☐ ☐ The major difference between survivor guilt and grief other than, "It was my fault"?

☐ ☐ The 10 trauma-specific intervention tasks drawing accomplishes?

☐ ☐ A minimum of 8 commonly expressed beliefs victims hold?

☐ ☐ A minimum of 8 commonly expressed beliefs of a survivor?

☐ ☐ A minimum of 15 different statements about trauma you want to present every parent of a traumatized child?

☐ ☐ 8 specific intervention needs of traumatized children?

☐ ☐ 10 trauma-specific goals of intervention?

☐ ☐ 12 factors parents should consider when looking for a good trauma specialist for their child?

☐ ☐ A minimum of 15 guidelines for survivors of suicide?

☐ ☐ 10 commonly heard expressions from children traumatized by suicide?

☐ ☐ 3 legal responsibilities when working with a potentially suicidal youth under seventeen years of age?

☐ ☐ 10 high risk factors other than specifics of a suicide plan which indicate that the individual experiencing any one of these risk factors has a high probability of attempting?

☐ ☐ 10 factors found in the profile of a suicidal individual?

☐ ☐ A minimum of 15 ways for parents to help their traumatized adolescent?

☐ ☐ 10 commonly heard expressions from children traumatized by a non-violent yet trauma inducing incident?

YES	NO	
☐	☐	The major differences between grief, bereavement, acute stress, traumatic stress, and PTSD?
☐	☐	Four specific drawings any traumatized child needs to be asked to draw?
☐	☐	The difference between implicit and explicit memory?
☐	☐	Two methods which allow a traumatized child to make us a witness to their experience?
☐	☐	Can you identify 5 procedures and list them in priority for intervening with students fighting (no weapons involved)?
☐	☐	Can you identify 5 procedures and list them in priority for dealing with an irate or potentially violent adult/parent?
☐	☐	Can you identify 15 do's and don't when confronted with a student/staff/parent with a weapon?

Have you been trained . . .

YES	NO	
☐	☐	In trauma-specific intervention techniques which utilizes both implicit and explicit memory functions?
☐	☐	To debrief and defuse those children, adolescents, and adults most-exposed to critical incidents using developmentally appropriate models?
☐	☐	Can you state the general rule for determining how many team members you will need on site following a critical incident?
☐	☐	Present a 30 minute oral summary of what you would say to students following a suicide death of a classmate?
☐	☐	Present a 30 minute oral summary of what you would say to students following a murder of a classmate specific to violent trauma?
☐	☐	Present a 30 minute oral summary of what you would say to students following a non-violent trauma such as a house fire, drowning or car fatality?

Scoring Part 2 (36 possible)

Score one point for each yes answer. To determine your percentage divide 36 into your score.
(Example: If you scored 12 yes answers, divide 12 by 36 for a score of 33%)

My Score:_____ My Percentage:_____%

Part 3 - Debriefing: Instructions

To be completed by all professionals in school or agency settings who are responsible for intervening with potentially traumatized children. Answer **YES** or **NO** to each question. If you are unsure as to whether or not you can accurately answer **YES** to a question, mark that question **NO**.

Part 3 - Debriefing: Readiness

YES   NO

☐   ☐   Do your debriefing formats accommodate for students developmentally, for system limitations, for staff size?

☐   ☐   Do you have a debriefing format for K-5th grade (defusing)?

☐   ☐   Do you have a different format for debriefing in a 45 minute session designed for all staff at the end of the day (Operational Debriefing)?

☐   ☐   Can you describe what forms of debriefing could be used with K-5th grade children?

☐   ☐   Do you have a format for debriefing the staff related to the effectiveness of the crisis team?

☐   ☐   Do yo have a release form developed for all students you select to participate in debriefing?

☐   ☐   Can you point out what factors would delay a debriefing beyond it's normal initiation following a critical incident?

☐   ☐   Do you have laminated debriefing cards for each model to insure the debriefing process is consistent and appropriately used?

☐   ☐   As part of your debriefing kit do yo have prepared handout materials for parents, specific activities for children in grades K-5 designed to restore their sense of safety?

☐   ☐   If you were asked to debrief a group of ten-to-twenty, or even thirty people, do you know... A) What opening statements are critical to include? B), What six questions you would ask?

☐   ☐   Can you list the four functions the administrator of the staff you are debriefing must be prepared to carry out?

☐   ☐   In preparing for a debriefing, what four responsibilities must the administration of the staff being debriefed be willing to assume?

☐   ☐   Can you describe how to prepare a room for debriefing?

☐   ☐   Can you identify the issues that are often problematic in agency settings, but not in school settings?

☐   ☐   Can you describe what criteria to use to determine who might need debriefing?

☐   ☐   Can a debriefing be made mandatory?

☐   ☐   Can you answer what a debriefer must do at the end of the debriefing before doing anything else or before meeting with anyone else?

☐   ☐   If your administrator presented you with an article that said debriefing was harmful, that continually talking about what happened was potentially dangerous, could you point out the specific weakness in the arguments of those who have been advocating that repression (not talking about it) is better?

Scoring Part 3 (18 Possible)

Score one point for each yes answer. To determine your percentage divide 18 into your score. (Example: If you scored 9 yes answers, divide 9 by 18 for a score of 50%)

My Score:_____   My Percentage:_____%

Part 4 · Protocol/Resource Readiness: Instructions

To be completed by crisis team members/administrators who are responsible for protocol and resources. Answer **YES** or **NO** to each question. If you are unsure as to whether or not you can accurately answer **YES** to a question, mark that question **NO**. (Not an all inclusive listing)

Do you currently use or have available...

YES   NO

☐   ☐   A suicide lethality checklist form which includes the most highly correlated risk factors related to suicide potential e.g. poor impulse control, constricted thinking, etc..

☐   ☐   A PTSD assessment tool for ages six through seventeen?

☐   ☐   A PTSD tool which identifies specific trauma reactions present and the frequency in which they occur?

☐   ☐   A PTSD tool which also identifies the (DSM-IV) subcategory present trauma reactions fall under and the subcategory showing the highest frequency of occurring reactions?

☐   ☐   A pre-post tool to evaluate the results of your intervention efforts to reduce reactions?

☐   ☐   A structured trauma-specific parent intake interview tool?

☐   ☐   An 8 session trauma-specific, field tested, intervention model for use in schools or agencies which uses drawing and other trauma-specific activities for children and adolescents?

☐   ☐   An 8 session group program for traumatized children 6-12 years old for use in school or agency setting?

☐   ☐   A trauma-specific intervention program for pre-school aged children in either a group or an individual setting?

☐   ☐   A booklet for parents of traumatized children which details the differences between trauma and grief in concrete, behavioral, and illustrated format which also includes ways parents can respond to their traumatized child?

☐   ☐   A booklet of the same nature for children 6-12 years old?

☐   ☐   A booklet of the same nature for adolescents?

☐   ☐   An already prepared letter to send to parents in which only brief details need to be added related to the present incident?

☐   ☐   A similarly already prepared statement for the media?

☐   ☐   Prepared announcements for teachers to read to students?

☐   ☐   Behavioral Referral Checklist for staff to use as a guide for directing students to the crisis team?

☐   ☐   Prepared statements for the receptionist to use with incoming phone calls to provide information and guidelines to assist in "triaging" the needs of those calls/callers?

☐   ☐   Scripted 15-30 minute classroom presentation format with differing content related to the appropriate type of incidents (e.g. suicide versus murder versus accidental death, versus kidnapping, etc.)?

YES	NO	
☐	☐	Prepared "task lists" for each team member as addendum for special situations e.g. overturned bus situation, hostage situation, potentially suicidal student or staff person?
☐	☐	Prepared "Release of Liability" parent form for parents who refuse to accept recommendations related to their potentially suicidal child/teen?
☐	☐	A "Hold Harmless Agreement" with non-school property owners who's site you may need to use when evacuating students and staff?

Does your Crisis Plan Kit contain:

YES	NO	
☐	☐	Potentially suicidal student disposition form?
☐	☐	"Violent Incident Disposition" and "Threat Assessment" forms?
☐	☐	Task checklist forms covering protocols to be initiated/completed?

Have you updated your protocols to accommodate responses to terrorism? Should you be . .

YES	NO	
☐	☐	The targeted school?
☐	☐	Not the targeted school, but in the target area?
☐	☐	Neither the targeted school, nor in the targeted area?

Do your updated parent release forms now contain . .

YES	NO	
☐	☐	A section for recording who the child was released to and at what time?
☐	☐	Where the parent would take their child that is approximately one-half to one full hour away, if they are unable to go home, and the phone number of that backup location?
☐	☐	Other children that a parent is allowed to and/or has taken in order to remove them from further pending danger as quickly as possible?

Are you prepared by . . .

YES	NO	
☐	☐	Having three evacuation routes should one or the other not be accessible?
☐	☐	Having a predetermined site miles away from the school should the area need to be evacuated?
☐	☐	Having a written Memorandums of Agreement (MOA) with other school districts detailing how they would accommodate your students should your facility no longer be accessible?
☐	☐	Having staff assigned/licensed to drive school buses in the event of an emergency?

YES   NO

☐   ☐   Having all rooms identified in sequential order by reflective numbers above the doors and at ground level?

☐   ☐   Having an emergency kit that contains, for example, 30 gallon plastic bags?

☐   ☐   Having flip charts for every classroom directing staff as to immediate actions needed following varied incidents?

☐   ☐   Having color coded cards in each classroom that teachers can take with them to the evacuation site?

Scoring Part 4 (38 possible)

Score one point for each yes answer. To determine your percentage divide 38 into your score. Example: if your score was 27 correct answers, divide that by 38 for a score of 71 %

My Score:_____   My Percentage:_____

Record Your Total Score

How did you do? Record your score for each section below.

Part 1   Total correct: _____   Your Percentage: _____
Part 2   Total correct: _____   Your Percentage: _____
Part 3   Total correct: _____   Your Percentage: _____
Part 4   Total correct: _____   Your Percentage: _____

Summary

This is not, by any means, an all inclusive review, but it should help you identify strengths and weaknesses. TLC has available multiple resource materials and trainings that can assist you in your efforts to develop and maintain an effective, efficient, competent responses to "high level" as well as "low level" crisis situations

Appendix B
Sample Letter to Parents
and Parent Handouts

Sample Letter of Introduction to Parents

Dear _____,

As you know, we recently experienced _____. This is very upsetting for students. We would like to give you an opportunity to involve your son/daughter in a Trauma Debriefing (Defusing) meeting on _____ at _____. Attached you will find a description of what can happen when children are traumatized. We want to prevent such reactions and help children quickly recover if they are already experiencing any of these reactions.

We believe this meeting will be very beneficial for your child.

Should you have any questions please call me at _____ before _____.

You may also sign below, to give permission for your child to attend the Debriefing meeting.

Sincerely,

_____

_____

Parent Signature

What Parents Need to Know

Children are Exposed to:

- Car fatalities
- Suicide
- Drowning
- Sudden death
- House fires
- Terminal illness
- Murder
- Physical/sexual abuse
- Divorce, separation, adoption
- Critical injuries, difficult surgery...

Plane crashes, overturned school busses, floods, earthquakes, workplace violence, neighborhood violence, kidnapping, hostage taking.

Children are Vulnerable to Grief and Trauma-specific Reactions:

- as surviving victims
- as witnesses
- as loved ones, friends, peers of victim(s)
- because they go to the same school and live in the same community as the victim, OR
- because they have seen on television situations like the Oklahoma bombing, where the victims are like themselves in age, or because the tragedy happened in a school, day care center, or other environment similar to their own.

Any child old enough to laugh
is old enough to experience trauma.

75

What a Parent Needs to Know

Your child can be traumatized in the same way as an adult.

Your child experiences reactions similar to traumatized adults.

Post traumatic stress creates reactions that are in addition to and different from grief.

Your child does not need to be a victim or a witness, but only related to a friend or peer, to be traumatized themselves.

Violence is not the only kind of incident that can induce trauma in your child.

Car accidents, house fires, serious surgical procedures, terminal illness of a loved one, drowning accident, finding a body, divorce, separation from a parent, plane crashes, floods, hurricanes can all induce trauma in a child.

A family trauma such as a murder of a family member can traumatize the entire family.

Each member of a family will have his/her own individual reactions.

Reactions may be more intense for some and less for others. The longer trauma victims go without trauma-specific help the more chronic and severe the reactions can become.

Trauma reactions cannot be prevented, but their negative impact on your child's learning, behavior, personality and emotional development can be minimized when help is provided as soon as possible.

Your child, when given an opportunity, will generally be eager and able to face the details of his trauma.

Trauma-specific help can assist your child in finding relief from his terror as well as regaining a sense of control and power over the "monsters" their experience created.

Your child, when taken for trauma-specific help, will be forever grateful to you, for acknowledging his need to talk with someone who understands what his terror is like.

A traumatized child desperately needs your patience, the feeling of safety, security and basic nurturing.

As a parent you, too will need information about ways trauma changes your child, and how you can best assist his recovery.

When Should I Be Concerned?
Terror On Top of Grief • Trauma Reactions in Children

Trauma reactions are different from grief reactions. Only recently has it been verified that children are vulnerable to experiencing Posttraumatic Stress Disorder (PTSD), a disorder once attributed to only adult survivors of war. These reactions appear in children following disasters, acts of violence, sudden unanticipated death, critical injuries, car fatalities, house fires, drownings and sudden unexpected incidents involving family or friends.

The one word that best describes grief is sadness; the one word that best describes trauma is terror. Terror induces reactions not often seen in children who are grieving. You should be concerned when your child has:

- trouble sleeping, afraid to sleep alone or be left alone even for short periods of time.
- is easily startled (terrorized) by sounds, sights, smells similar to those that existed at the time of the event - a car backfiring may sound like the gun shot that killed someone; for one child, his dog pouncing down the stairs brought back the sound of his father falling down the stairs and dying.
- becomes hypervigilant - forever watching out for and anticipating that they are, about to be, or are, in danger.
- seeks safety "spots" in their environment, in whatever room they may be in at the time. Children who sleep on the floor instead of in their bed after a trauma do so because they fear the comfort of a bed will let them sleep so hard they won't hear the danger coming.
- becomes irritable, aggressive, acting tough, provoking fights.
- verbalizes a desire for revenge.
- acts as if they are no longer afraid of anything or anyone, and in the face of danger, responding inappropriately, verbalizing that nothing ever scares them anymore.
- forgets recently acquired skills.
- returns to behaviors they had previously stopped i.e. bed wetting, nail biting, or developing disturbing behaviors such as stuttering.
- withdraws and wants less to do with their friends.
- develops headaches, stomach problems, fatigue, and/or other ailments not previously present.
- becomes accident prone, taking risks they had previously avoided, putting themselves in life threatening situations, reenacting the event as a victim and/or a hero.
- develops school problems including a drop in grades and difficulty concentrating.
- develops a pessimistic view of the future, losing their resilience to overcome additional difficulties, losing hope, losing their passion to survive, play and enjoy life.

While these changes are not unusual, they often go unnoticed or fail to bring a helping response from adults. These changes can and do become permanent when the child does not receive appropriate help. Often children suffer silently for years with their terror until one or several of these changes become so intense and problematic that someone says something. Unfortunately, years later few people are likely to associate these reactions to the child's earlier trauma. The help given often misses the mark. This further increases the child's sense of helplessness and failure.

Ways to Help Your Child
and Help Yourself At the Same Time

Understand

1) Trauma is like no other experience. It brings out reactions you may have never seen before, nor your child has ever experienced.
2) Your child may not have control over his behavior because the terror he experienced has left him feeling out of control. It may be that terror which is driving his behaviors.
3) As long as a child's behavior is not hurting others or himself, it is okay.
4) If your child's behavior is upsetting to you, it is best to talk with a trauma specialist before reacting because these behaviors need special intervention.

Be Patient

1) Trauma destroys a child's sense of safety and security. He will need time to feel safe again and to feel that you can protect him.
2) As a parent of a traumatized child, it will be very difficult to see your child return to behaviors he engaged in years earlier, to see him act entirely different than the child you knew him to be before the trauma. He needs you to be patient.
3) Whatever behaviors he turns to after the trauma, no matter how strange or frightening they are for you, it is your child's attempt to feel powerful and safe again. Be patient. Do not push them to change or to stop until you have consulted a trauma specialist.

Be Nurturing

1) Whatever the age, any trauma needs to be followed by a lot of nurturing.
2) Let your child eat whatever he wants, follow you around or even withdraw for a while. Your child may want to be taken care of, to have fewer demands.
3) Spend more time with your child the first several weeks.

Keep It Simple

1) A terrorized child, adolescent, or adult will find it difficult to concentrate and remember even the simplest of things.
2) A terrorized individual will be forgetful. He can even forget what he was doing or talking about five minutes earlier.
3) You need to simplify everything for several weeks. Do not expect more. Do not introduce new challenges. This is a time to protect your child from stress. It really needs to be an, "all the cookies and milk I want," time for traumatized children.

Normalize

1) Reinforce that you understand that his reactions are not unusual following his experience.
2) Learn what trauma reactions can be expected and let your child know what he may yet experience.

Sample Follow-Up Letter to Parents

This letter can be placed in the computer and changes made according to the issue/sessions(s) it addresses. The follow-up letter can be used after each session or minimally after every two sessions. By sending information to the parent following sessions, you are more likely to engage the parents support. Parents generally are not accustomed to such attention as well as involvement. Your efforts will be appreciated.

Dear _____,

_____ has completed the Debriefing (Defusing)
Session(s) _____. In these sessions we focused
specifically on _____. I am not sure
what _____ has told you about the session, if anything, but I
want you to know that he/she is responding.

In our next sessions (optional) we will be dealing with_____.
If you have any questions or concerns please call me immediately at _____.

What has impressed me the most since we last communicated is _____.

As always, if there are any critical concerns I will call you immediately to arrange an appointment, or if needed, discuss the situation by phone.

Thank you again for your continued support. Simply allowing _____ the opportunity to participate in this session allows him/her to know you care.

Thank you again.

Sincerely,

NOTE: The purpose of such feedback is to maintain a connection with the parent and hopefully engage their support when it is most needed. The letter therefore needs to remain positive and brief. If there are major concerns you need to contact the parents by phone.

Appendix C
Comorbidity Chart
Trauma-specific Reaction Subcategories
Factors Potentially Prolonging Trauma
Victim-Survivor Thinking
Suicide Lethality Checklist

PTSD Chart
Comorbidity and Differential Diagnosis

Dr. Marquita Bedway, Children's Hospital of Detroit developed the Comorbidity and Differential Diagnosis Chart for the TLC Institute. It compares PTSD reactions with other disorders such as 1) anxiety spectrum disorders, 2) generalized anxiety disorder, 3) acute stress disorder, 4) obsessive compulsive disorder, 5) depressive disorder, 6) ADHD and 7) personality disorders.

It is quite common to misinterpret trauma reactions for psychopathology, especially if the psychologist is unfamiliar with posttraumatic symptomatology. Unless there is documentation of pre-existing disorders in the child, it should be presumed that the reactions are not the result of unconscious conflicts, but rather of **the overwhelming terror and the collapse of coping mechanisms in response to trauma.** These reactions should be seen as **expected responses** to a terrifying physical and psychic crisis.

Reactions Resulting From Trauma

PTSD can also induce other disorders when interventions are not successful in managing PTSD reactions. (see chart)

A variety of symptoms such as those in depression, suicidal ideation, attention disorders, conduct disturbances, increased aggression, phobic behaviors, obsessive compulsive behaviors, and panic disorder can emerge following a traumatic experience. All can be fueled by posttraumatic reactions.

Too often, exploration of a previous trauma inducing incident is ignored when the above reactions present themselves. Obviously, interventions which do not address previous trauma involvement are going to be less effective. When attention to trauma is provided, even if that trauma occurred years earlier, it is not unusual to see the reduction of such symptoms.

Diagnosis is not always easy, but too often PTSD in children goes undiagnosed and mistaken for other disorders. This chart helps simplify the differences, as well as similarities, among the disorders.

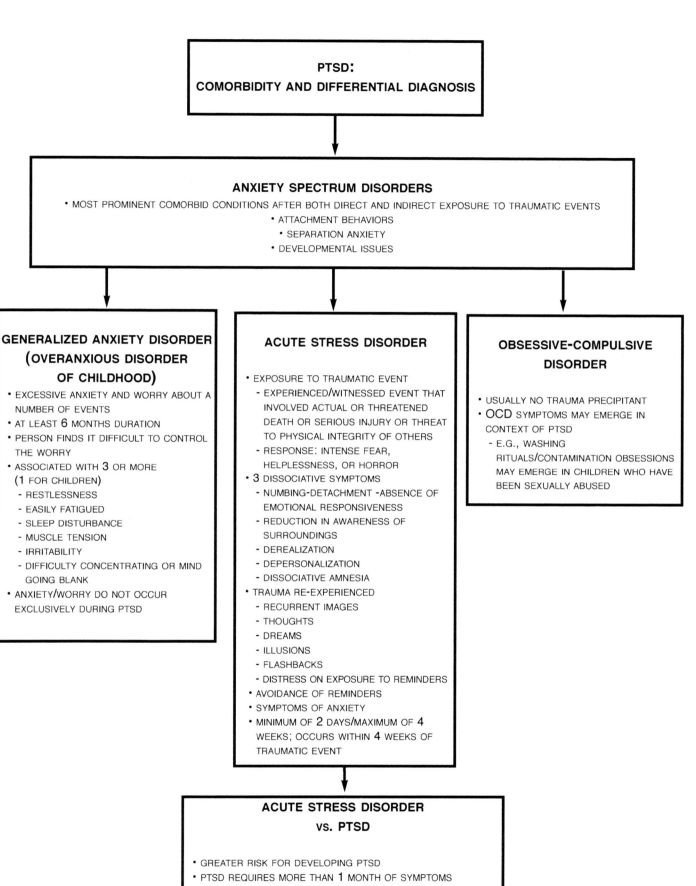

PTSD:
COMORBIDITY AND DIFFERENTIAL DIAGNOSIS

ANXIETY SPECTRUM DISORDERS
- MOST PROMINENT COMORBID CONDITIONS AFTER BOTH DIRECT AND INDIRECT EXPOSURE TO TRAUMATIC EVENTS
- ATTACHMENT BEHAVIORS
- SEPARATION ANXIETY
- DEVELOPMENTAL ISSUES

GENERALIZED ANXIETY DISORDER (OVERANXIOUS DISORDER OF CHILDHOOD)
- EXCESSIVE ANXIETY AND WORRY ABOUT A NUMBER OF EVENTS
- AT LEAST 6 MONTHS DURATION
- PERSON FINDS IT DIFFICULT TO CONTROL THE WORRY
- ASSOCIATED WITH 3 OR MORE (1 FOR CHILDREN)
  - RESTLESSNESS
  - EASILY FATIGUED
  - SLEEP DISTURBANCE
  - MUSCLE TENSION
  - IRRITABILITY
  - DIFFICULTY CONCENTRATING OR MIND GOING BLANK
- ANXIETY/WORRY DO NOT OCCUR EXCLUSIVELY DURING PTSD

ACUTE STRESS DISORDER
- EXPOSURE TO TRAUMATIC EVENT
  - EXPERIENCED/WITNESSED EVENT THAT INVOLVED ACTUAL OR THREATENED DEATH OR SERIOUS INJURY OR THREAT TO PHYSICAL INTEGRITY OF OTHERS
  - RESPONSE: INTENSE FEAR, HELPLESSNESS, OR HORROR
- 3 DISSOCIATIVE SYMPTOMS
  - NUMBING-DETACHMENT -ABSENCE OF EMOTIONAL RESPONSIVENESS
  - REDUCTION IN AWARENESS OF SURROUNDINGS
  - DEREALIZATION
  - DEPERSONALIZATION
  - DISSOCIATIVE AMNESIA
- TRAUMA RE-EXPERIENCED
  - RECURRENT IMAGES
  - THOUGHTS
  - DREAMS
  - ILLUSIONS
  - FLASHBACKS
  - DISTRESS ON EXPOSURE TO REMINDERS
- AVOIDANCE OF REMINDERS
- SYMPTOMS OF ANXIETY
- MINIMUM OF 2 DAYS/MAXIMUM OF 4 WEEKS; OCCURS WITHIN 4 WEEKS OF TRAUMATIC EVENT

OBSESSIVE-COMPULSIVE DISORDER
- USUALLY NO TRAUMA PRECIPITANT
- OCD SYMPTOMS MAY EMERGE IN CONTEXT OF PTSD
  - E.G., WASHING RITUALS/CONTAMINATION OBSESSIONS MAY EMERGE IN CHILDREN WHO HAVE BEEN SEXUALLY ABUSED

ACUTE STRESS DISORDER vs. PTSD
- GREATER RISK FOR DEVELOPING PTSD
- PTSD REQUIRES MORE THAN 1 MONTH OF SYMPTOMS
- IF SYMPTOMS PERSIST MORE THAN 1 MONTH, DIAGNOSE PTSD

Prepared by Dr. Marquita Bedway, Children's Hospital of Detroit, 1996

William Steele

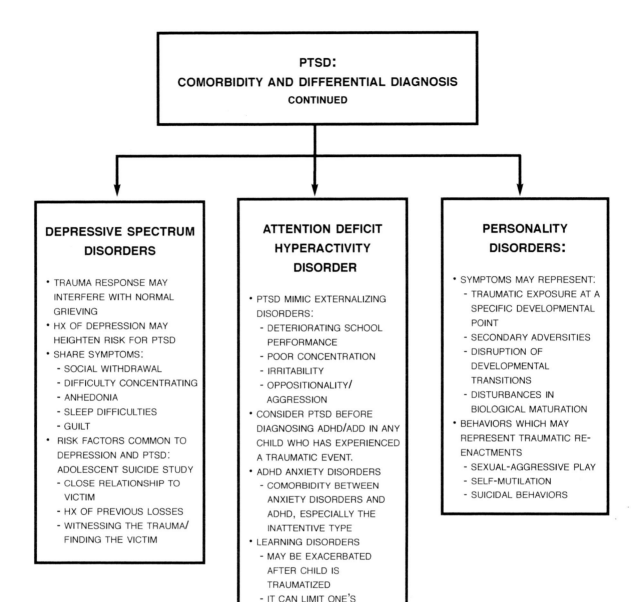

PTSD:
COMORBIDITY AND DIFFERENTIAL DIAGNOSIS
CONTINUED

DEPRESSIVE SPECTRUM
DISORDERS

- TRAUMA RESPONSE MAY
  INTERFERE WITH NORMAL
  GRIEVING
- HX OF DEPRESSION MAY
  HEIGHTEN RISK FOR PTSD
- SHARE SYMPTOMS:
  - SOCIAL WITHDRAWAL
  - DIFFICULTY CONCENTRATING
  - ANHEDONIA
  - SLEEP DIFFICULTIES
  - GUILT
- RISK FACTORS COMMON TO
  DEPRESSION AND PTSD:
  ADOLESCENT SUICIDE STUDY
  - CLOSE RELATIONSHIP TO
    VICTIM
  - HX OF PREVIOUS LOSSES
  - WITNESSING THE TRAUMA/
    FINDING THE VICTIM

ATTENTION DEFICIT
HYPERACTIVITY
DISORDER

- PTSD MIMIC EXTERNALIZING
  DISORDERS:
  - DETERIORATING SCHOOL
    PERFORMANCE
  - POOR CONCENTRATION
  - IRRITABILITY
  - OPPOSITIONALITY/
    AGGRESSION
- CONSIDER PTSD BEFORE
  DIAGNOSING ADHD/ADD IN ANY
  CHILD WHO HAS EXPERIENCED
  A TRAUMATIC EVENT.
- ADHD ANXIETY DISORDERS
  - COMORBIDITY BETWEEN
    ANXIETY DISORDERS AND
    ADHD, ESPECIALLY THE
    INATTENTIVE TYPE
- LEARNING DISORDERS
  - MAY BE EXACERBATED
    AFTER CHILD IS
    TRAUMATIZED
  - IT CAN LIMIT ONE'S
    PROCESSING OF THE
    TRAUMATIC EVENT

PERSONALITY
DISORDERS:

- SYMPTOMS MAY REPRESENT:
  - TRAUMATIC EXPOSURE AT A
    SPECIFIC DEVELOPMENTAL
    POINT
  - SECONDARY ADVERSITIES
  - DISRUPTION OF
    DEVELOPMENTAL
    TRANSITIONS
  - DISTURBANCES IN
    BIOLOGICAL MATURATION
- BEHAVIORS WHICH MAY
  REPRESENT TRAUMATIC RE-
  ENACTMENTS
  - SEXUAL-AGGRESSIVE PLAY
  - SELF-MUTILATION
  - SUICIDAL BEHAVIORS

PTSD

REEXPERIENCING
- INTRUSIVE THOUGHTS, FEELINGS
- TRAUMATIC DREAMS
- DISSOCIATIVE FLASHBACKS
- INTENSE PSYCHOLOGICAL DISTRESS
- PHYSIOLOGICAL REACTIVITY

PERSISTENT AVOIDANCE
- OF THOUGHTS, FEELINGS, TALKING
- ACTIVITIES, PLACES, PEOPLE
- INABILITY TO RECALL
- DETACHMENT, ESTRANGEMENT
- RESTRICTED AFFECT
- FORESHORTENED FUTURE

INCREASED AROUSAL
- SLEEP DIFFICULTY
- IRRITABILITY, ASSAULTIVE
- DIFFICULTY CONCENTRATING
- HYPERVIGILANCE
- STARTLE RESPONSE

Prepared by Dr. Marquita Bedway, Children's Hospital of Detroit, 1996

Re-experiencing the Trauma

Should you experience any of these reactions beyond the initial four week period following the incident, please call us immediately.

The traumatic event is persistently reexperienced in at least one of the following ways:

1. Recurrent, intrusive, distressing recollections of the event, including images, thoughts, or perceptions.
2. Recurrent, distressing dreams of the event.
3. Acting or feeling as if the traumatic event were recurring (includes a sense of reliving the experience, illusions, hallucinations, and dissociative flashback episodes, including those that occur upon awakening or when intoxicated).
4. Intense psychological distress at exposure to internal cues that symbolize or resemble an aspect of the traumatic event. Fear, anxiety and anger are possible examples.
5. Physiologic reactivity upon exposure to internal or external cues that symbolize or resemble an aspect of the traumatic event. Nausea, difficulty breathing and faintness are some possible examples.

Numbing and Avoidance

Persistent avoidance of stimuli associated with the trauma or numbing of general responsiveness (not present before the trauma).

1. Efforts to avoid thoughts, feelings, or conversations associated with the trauma.
2. Efforts to avoid activities, places, or people that arouse recollections of the trauma.
3. Inability to recall an important aspect of the trauma.
4. Markedly diminished interest or participation in significant activities.
5. Feeling of detachment or estrangement from others.
6. Restricted range of affect (e.g., unable to have loving feelings).
7. Sense of a foreshortened future (e.g., does not expect to have a career, marriage, or children, or a normal life span) (DSM-IV).

Hyperarousal
and Persistent Symptoms of Increased Arousal

(not present before the trauma - see note)

1. Difficulty falling or staying asleep.
2. Irritability or outbursts of anger.
3. Difficulty concentrating.
4. Hypervigilance.
5. Exaggerated startle response.

Reactions may extend beyond the four week acute stress period when a person is involved in disasters or other external events where physical reminders cannot be avoided. The same may occur when the details of an incident are kept alive in the media for an extended period of time.

Should any of these symptoms persist beyond a 4-8 week period and/or emerge as delayed reactions months later, we strongly recommend consultation with a trauma consultant.

NOTE: Trauma can induce biological and neurological changes which play a part in the ability to sleep, levels of anxiety, concentration, and other trauma-specific reactions. Should reactions persist beyond the four week period, consultation for temporary medication should be considered. The loss of sleep, intrusive thoughts, anxiety and other reactions induced by trauma can deplete an individual of much needed physical rest and inner emotional calmness and precipitate yet more problems for the individual. Medication, at times, is simply a necessity.

(gathered from the APA - DSM-IV)

Factors Placing Traumatized Children At Risk
&
Factors Potentially Prolonging Trauma Reactions

Factors Placing Individuals at Risk

Factors which place trauma victims at risk for additional and more intense reactions include:

1) The terrifying effects of the suddenness of an unexpected event
2) The threat to life
3) The degree to which the individual feels helpless and powerless
4) The physical proximity to the trauma
5) Duration of exposure to the terrifying elements of the event, i.e. violence, dismemberment, mutilation, destruction of the body
6) Visually graphic and grotesque details
7) Continuous exposure via media, lengthy judicial procedures, physical reminders
8) Loss of support
9) Survivor guilt

Factors Potentially Prolonging Trauma Reactions

Factors following a traumatic experience which have the potential to prolong trauma reactions, as well as place the individual at risk for more serious symptomatology include:

1) Additional traumatic exposure, i.e. domestic violence, community violence or simply ongoing exposure due to physical reminders, media, lengthy judicial proceedings, etc.
2) A dysfunctional parent unable to provide consistent nurturing and protection from harm or the threat of harm
3) Pre-existing disorders
4) Absence of a safe environment
5) Limited social support system or perceived lack of support
6) Assumption of victim thinking (see next page)
7) Additional secondary losses, i.e. loss of friends or familiar surroundings, secondary victimization by caregivers and caretakers
8) Ongoing legal issues, such as in the case of murder, the trial, etc.
9) Significant hormonal/biochemical changes induced by the trauma which trigger physiological, emotional and cognitive changes necessitating medication
10) Absence of accessibility to trauma-specific intervention

Victim Thinking

Following are statements reflective of individuals who think and behave as victims. (Matsakis, *Aphrodite: Post-Traumatic Stress Disorder*, New Harbinger Publications, Inc., CA. 1994)

To begin, check the boxes beside those statements that sound like something you find yourself thinking or feeling.

☐ I have to accept bad situations because they are part of life and I can do nothing to make them better.

☐ I don't expect much good to happen in my life.

☐ Nobody could ever love me.

☐ I am always going to feel sad, angry, depressed, and confused.

☐ There are situations at work and at home that I could do something about, but I don't have the motivation to do so.

☐ Life overwhelms me, so I prefer to be alone whenever possible.

☐ You can't trust anyone except a few people.

☐ I feel I have to be extra good, competent, and attractive in order to compensate for my many defects.

☐ I feel guilty for many things, even things that I know are not my fault.

☐ I feel I have to explain myself to people so that they will understand me. But sometimes I get tired of explaining, conclude it's not worth the effort, and stay alone.

☐ I'm often afraid to do something new for fear I will make a mistake.

☐ I can't afford to be wrong.

☐ I feel that when people look at me, they know right away that I'm different.

☐ Sometimes I think that those who died during the traumatic event I experienced were better off than me. At least they don't have to live with the memories.

☐ I am afraid of the future.

☐ Most times I think things will never get better. There is not much I can do to make my life better.

☐ I can be either a perfectionist or a total slob depending on my mood.

☐ I tend to see people as either for me or against me.

☐ I feel pressure to go along with others, even when I don't want to. To avoid such pressures, I avoid people.

☐ I am never going to get over what happened to me.

☐ I find myself apologizing for myself to others.

☐ I have very few choices in life.

Survivor Thinking

Developed by TLC Institute
(check those which apply)

☐ Yes, bad situations come up in my life but I can do things to make them better.

☐ I expect a lot of good to happen in my life.

☐ I am loveable and people love me.

☐ I may feel sad, angry, depressed and confused today, but I will not always feel this way. Things will get better.

☐ I have a lot to offer the world and I am motivated to go forward.

☐ I am capable. I handle life with confidence.

☐ I have people I can trust.

☐ I am a worthy person. I have many traits that are worthwhile.

☐ I am only responsible for myself. I cannot control everything.

☐ Those who can, will like me and understand me without a lot of explaining or apologizing.

☐ Everyone makes mistakes; that is how we learn.

☐ It is okay to be wrong. I am still a good person.

☐ People see me in a positive way.

☐ I take each day as it comes.

☐ I look forward to the future.

☐ I am in control of my life. There are things I can do to make my life better.

☐ My life is balanced.

☐ People are supportive of me. I trust my inner self to make good choices about others.

☐ I am strong. I face difficult situations head on.

☐ Each day I get a little stronger. I will get over this.

☐ I am a survivor. I need not apologize. I am surviving.

☐ As a survivor, I have many choices in my life.

Suicide Lethality Checklist

Traumatization can lead to suicidal ideation and eventual attempt. It is important to be able to identify potentially suicidal children/adolescents and know how to intervene with them.

Certainly you should be skilled in an initial assessment of risk if the child/adolescent indicates some suicidal processes. The Lethality Checklist on the next page is only meant to be a guide. Hopefully it will alert you to the need for additional evaluation.

Risk Assessment

What happens when youngsters say "yes" to your question, " Have you thought about killing yourself?" The immediate task is to assess the possible risk involved. This necessitates asking very specific questions. You need to know if they have thought about how they would kill themselves. The more specific the plan, the higher the risk. If they have a when, where, and how, it is serious. It is necessary to ascertain if the means is available to them - for example, is there a gun in the house? If the means is available, the risk is greater. Find out if they are using drugs; there is a 50% correlation between suicide and drugs. In addition to these factors, if there is a history of suicide in the family, and/or one of the parents has been chronically depressed, the risk is greater still. If someone they know has recently completed suicide, the risk is higher. When the suicidal person is focused solely on dying as a solution (tunnel vision) and cannot attach himself to any future possibility, the risk may be higher.

This tunnel vision is often expressed by using words like *always, never,* and *either/or, It will always be this way, It will never change, Either I make this relationship work or I'll kill myself.* Other high-risk factors include history of physical/sexual victimization, witness to violence and poor impulse control. Regardless of whether the suicide is deemed low-risk, a child with a history of poor impulse control who is thinking about suicide is, in fact, a very high-risk as he may lack the ability to think things through and act on their thoughts. Homosexual preference is also a risk factor.

Be aware that when assessing risk, the higher the number of risk factors present, the higher the risk. This does not mean, however, that if only a few of the risk factors are present there is little likelihood of an attempt. Someone who has no plan, only an ideation, but is drinking alcohol, could be considered high risk. We strongly recommend a second opinion by another member of your crisis team and/or by an outside referral source. **The determination of risk and any subsequent interventions, should not be the responsibility of one person.**

Suicide Lethality Checklist for Youth

PART I (All High Risk Factors)	LOW	MODERATE	HIGH
Plan	___ none	___ vague	___ specific*
	*What is the plan? _____		
Method	What is method? _____		
Method available	___ no		___ yes
When	___ unplanned	___ vague	___ specific
Where	___ unplanned	___ vague	___ specific
Previous attempt	___ no		___ yes
Alcohol/drug use	___ none	___ sporadic	___ chronic
Recent loss	___ none		___ yes

PART II (*Highest Risk Factors)	LOW	MODERATE	HIGH
*Physical assault	___ no	___ recent	___ ongoing
*Sexual assault	___ no	___ recent	___ ongoing
*Witness to violent behavior/trauma	___ no	___ recent	___ ongoing
*Beating/humiliation by others	___ no	___ recent	___ ongoing
Hyposomnia/Disturbed sleep	___ no	___ recent	___ ongoing
Preoccupied with death/dying	___ no	___ recent	___ ongoing
*Gender identity issues	___ no	___ recent	___ ongoing
*Poor impulse control	___ no	___ recent	___ ongoing
*Fear of losing control	___ no	___ recent	___ ongoing
Loss of concentration	___ no	___ recent	___ ongoing
Psychomotor retardation/agitation	___ no	___ recent	___ ongoing
*Constricted thinking	___ no	___ recent	___ ongoing
Somatic complaints	___ no	___ recent	___ ongoing
*Expression of guilt/shame	___ no	___ recent	___ ongoing
*Expression of hopelessness	___ no	___ recent	___ ongoing
*Chronically depressed parent	___ no		___ yes
*Turning against self (verbally)	___ no		___ yes
Perceived support of others	___ several supports	___ one/two	___ none
*Refuses to contract	___ no		___ yes
TOTAL	___	___	___

Appendix D
Classroom Presentation Outline
Review Chapter Eight for Details of Process

<u>NOTE</u>: Conducting classroom presentations demands a working knowledge of survivor reactions following different trauma inducing incidents. Reactions after suicide are different from reactions following a murder, kidnapping, etc. Reactions to these events will be somewhat different than reactions to accidental (non-violent) deaths such as car fatalities. Trauma reactions differ from grief reactions. You need to know these differences in order to normalize them. Space does not allow for a detailed description of these differences.

TLC recommended resources for this information include *Trauma Response Protocol Manual For Schools, Structured Sensory Interventions for Children, Adolescents and Parents (SITCAP)*. TLC's Certification Program also provides extensive coverage of these differences. (See Appendix E for these and other resources.)

Classroom Presentations

Outline

The following outline can be used regardless of the type of incident. We strongly recommend that a core group of staff be trained to assist team members in conducting classroom presentations so all students can be reached within the first two days. Immediate presentations help diffuse unwanted student responses. A core group of twelve staff (2 per class) can cover most classes in two days.

This outline does not include the different reactions survivors may have following different types of incidents such as: suicide, murder, non-violent trauma, grief, etc. Each situation will dictate a change in content presented. We recommend several TLC resources for this information; *Trauma Response Protocol Manual For Schools, Structured Sensory Interventions for Children, Adolescents and Parents (SITCAP)*. (See suggested resources in Appendix H.)

1. Introduction

This is very difficult for us all. It is not easy to know what to say or how to act. Sometimes our own reactions frighten us because they are so new to us or seem so strong.

We are here with your teacher to talk about _____, to answer your questions if we can and to tell you of some of the reactions you may have that are very normal.

2. Beginning

This is what we know so far _____.

Have any of you heard anything different about (the way he/she died, was killed, injured, kidnapped, etc.)?

Did any of you play/spend time with or have conversations with _____ in the past couple of weeks? Tell us about that. What do you remember?

Have any of you had a similar incident happen to a family member or friend?

What upsets you most about _____ 's (death, murder, injury, etc.)?

What questions do you have about what happened or even about what will be happening over the next few days?

3. Normalize

Let us describe the kinds of reactions that most people have following this kind of situation. (Use appropriate survivor reactions i.e. suicide, homicide, trauma. Briefly identify and explain the possible reactions and then relate the following.)

You may already have experienced some of these reactions or you may experience them weeks, even months, from now. They are very normal reactions so do not be alarmed. It will help, however, if you can talk to someone about them.

4. Identifying Appropriate Behavior

This will vary somewhat depending upon the incident. If the incident is suicide, the students need to clearly hear what they are to do if a friend talks about ending his/her life. (For specific content, *Trauma Response Protocol Manual For Schools* is recommended.) *If the incident is murder, then messages about revenge are critical,* and so on...

Basic Expectations Students Need to Hear

This is a time when it is not unusual for us to look for reasons why this happened. A lot of rumors can get started that are not at all helpful to the family or to close friends. If you hear stories that are different from the information we give you, please let us know so we can check them out, correct them, or confirm them.

Sometimes we want to blame others. This is normal but not something we want to do. It simply doesn't help and can, in fact, cause the person or persons being blamed to retaliate (want to fight back) and that doesn't help anyone.

Although it is very normal to be angry, it is not acceptable to seek revenge on those we think may be the cause of _____ 's death. We simply will not accept anyone going after anyone else.

Sometimes situations like this cause us to ask many questions we never thought of before. It is important that you ask the questions. Some of your questions may be personal. You can certainly feel free to ask any one of us or your teacher. This is how you can reach us...

Add additional issues specific to your situation as needed. (Again, *Trauma Response Protocol For Schools* is recommended for its varied content.)

5. Conclusion

Ask, "Are there any other questions before we end? If at any time over the next several days you want to talk with someone, let your teacher know and we'll be contacted - or come and see us directly. Here are the names of the other staff on the trauma response team who can help..."

NOTE: Be prepared for silence. Students may not always know what to say or ask. They may not initially give you credibility or simply be so overwhelmed they can only listen.

If students do not respond to your initial questions ask and then answer the questions you anticipated students might have asked.

You may wish to express some of your own personal reactions initially, this sometimes give students "permission" to open up also.

Inform students of the related activities which are planned over the next several days, that they will be kept informed of new information and upcoming activities.

The classroom presentation may be as short as 25 minutes or last the entire class period with very vocal students. The important fact is that you are there trying to help. That makes you human and can help diffuse student anger and acting out when staff do not sit down with students face to face. (The assembly method simply is not as effective as smaller classroom presentations.)

NOTE: If you are responding to a suicide it will be critical to be very direct with students about suicide being an unacceptable choice, what they might do if they have friends who are talking about it, etc. (The *Trauma Response Protocol Manual For Schools* text is highly recommended for its detailed descriptions of what students need to hear.)

We also recommend that classroom presentations be conducted by your own staff. Children in crisis look to their counselors, teachers, administrators for protection and help. Using outside sources frequently angers students, distances them from staff, "chips away" at their trust in staff.

Appendix E
Trauma Debriefing Model
Debriefing Debriefers Model
Individual Debriefing Format
Debriefing Handout Material

Trauma Debriefing for
Adults and Adolescents
Specifically in Schools or Agencies

Group Size: Eight to ten participants.

Group Membership: Debrief adolescents separate from adults. Debrief agency administrators, managers, and supervisors separate from line staff. Debrief crisis team members, including administrators of team separately from other staff. (The exception is schools, as detailed earlier.)

Session Length: Recommend maximum two hour duration.

Resource Materials: Felt marker, kleenex, hand outs and reference materials, card stock or plain paper to "tent" and write their first names on to set on the table in front of them.

Location: In house but in an area not to be utilized by others during the session.

Room Set up: Debriefing can be conducted around a table or in a circle without a table. One is not more beneficial than the other.

Seating Arrangement: Debriefers are to sit among participants rather than together so as to minimize an "Us - Them" perception.

Special Considerations: Coffee, tea, pop, water is permissible.
Phone needs to be disconnected or the <u>ringer turned off</u>. Beepers are to be put on vibration and/or turned off. It is understood that no one is to have access to the participants except for extreme emergency. Back up personnel must be assigned for those participants.

Administrative Responsibility: The Chief Administrator and/or designee must be present at the facility and immediately accessible during the debriefing process and following the process. The administrator's presence is necessary for three reasons: 1) a participant leaves during the session because it has become too difficult, the debriefer must physically bring that staff person to the administrator following the help provided to the participant; 2) problems arise which need immediate resolution; 3) requests for additional support and resources are made which can only be addressed by the administrator. (It is not the role of the debriefer to engage in problem solving system or personnel issues.)

Number of Debriefers: Three debriefers are recommended - one to lead each of the three stages of this model.

Debriefing Stages

Introductory Story Stage

This stage includes the introduction by the leader of the debriefers, the goals of debriefing, an orientation to its process, the ground rules, details of the participants exposure to the incident and their cognitive reactions to it.

Personal Reaction Stage

This stage includes the sharing of physical and emotional reactions experienced at the time of the incident up to this point in the session.

Summary Stage

This stage includes a review of information shared, normalization of reactions, education as to what additional reactions and issues may yet emerge, identification of problems specific to the response of others and/or need for additional support and resources, review of ways to care for self including of referral information.

Stage Assignment

Prior to beginning the session, one debriefer experienced in crisis intervention, must be assigned the role of following and intervening with any participant who leaves the session prematurely. A leader of the debriefing team must be determined and is responsible for consulting with the designated person administratively responsible for attending participants. The consultation involves site arrangements, participant back up coverage, supporting non-access to participants, faculty response to participant requests for possible additional support and/or need for immediate resolution of a problem area, the securing of incident detail which is then provided other debriefers prior to initiating the session.

The Script

Introductory Story Stage

The statements and questions detailed for each stage have been field-tested for clarity and for their ability to assist participants in the reconstruction of the information specific to the incident, the externalization of specific trauma reactions and the presentation of information critical to healing.

<u>NOTE</u>: For your convenience the following script is laid out so you can copy it and cut and paste it on 5" x 8" index cards. It may make it easier to use in this form.

The narrative portions may be adjusted to fit your style but must clearly communicate the intended message. **Do not alter the questions**. Altering the questions will minimize their impact, overgeneralize the focus, and lead to responses not specific to posttraumatic stress reactions.

Please reread Chapter Four to review process issues and specific questions before beginning.

To Start

Have participants take their seats. Arrange yourselves among participants. Complete name tags if not already completed. The leader of the debriefing teams begins.

Introduction

It is unfortunate that such a traumatic incident has brought us together. I'm sorry you have had to experience such a difficult thing.

Team Member Introductions

My name is _____. These are my colleagues _____ and _____. (You may provide a very brief statement about your experiences with debriefing.)

- We have been asked to meet with you to give you some information about trauma and all its possible reactions which are very likely new for you, but very normal reactions following these kinds of situations. We are here to pass on to you what others have experienced following similar incidents.

- We are also here to help you describe your experiences to one another. Even though some of you may not want to be here right now, we think you'll find that this will help you with what you have experienced, and help you see that you are probably sharing some similar reactions.

- This is not about how well you responded. It is about looking at all the kinds of reactions you are experiencing and may yet experience in the weeks to come. There is no right or wrong reaction. This is not about blaming; about what was done right or wrong. It is about learning what you need to know about trauma that can help you heal.   *1.*

- This session must be confidential. This means no one is to talk to anyone about anything that is said here today. You may tell others of your reactions but not what others talk about today. Do we all agree?

- We will start by asking you about your relationship to _____ (or what happened). Each of you will have an opportunity to respond as we go around the group. You may pass on a question but we will come back to you later. We will go in the same order for each question. After spending time on factual information and details, we will look at personal reactions. The last stage is the summary stage where we will give you some information, ways to help yourself. We will also give you the opportunity to make some recommendations as to what might be helpful for you in your workplace. Afterwards, your principal/administrator will join as briefly to respond to your recommendations.

- Listening to what one another has to say will be very helpful to healing and feeling better. We must ask that you not interrupt while one of the other participants is talking. Initially you will have many personal reactions that will cause you to want to say things in response to what you hear. What you feel is important and we will talk about personal reactions later in the meeting. However, until we get to that part we want to be talking about factual information.   *2.*

• You may notice that we have index cards. As you begin to tell your stories you will be making us, in a way, witnesses. It is sometimes difficult for us to listen to the details of such tragic situations. It is not easy for anyone. These cards list the questions we want to ask you so we can make sure we cover all the critical issues and give you the best help possible.

• Also _____ will be taking some notes to help when we get to the point where we give a review and a summary of all we have learned. There will be a lot said and we want to be sure to capture as much as we can. If taking notes is a problem, just let us know and we'll put the note pad away. When we are finished, we will rip up our notes. No records will be kept

• Just one last issue. If you have beepers/phones, could you please turn them off or place them on the silent mode. Back up staff have been assigned to cover for you, so there is no reason for interruption during this meeting. Is everyone okay with that. And, I believe you have been told that we will finish within two hours. The time varies with each situation, but we will not go beyond two hours. Let's begin....

3.

The questioning begins now
Let us begin with the factual information and details

1. First can you please tell us who you are and what your relationship is to _____ (victim). Allow each one to answer in order then continue.

2. Where were you when this happened or when you first found out and what did you do?

3. What stands out most in your mind as to what you might have seen, or heard when you arrived or when you first found out about it?

4. Are there details about what happened that you have heard since it happened, other than what others here have told us?

5. Was there anything that others have said that was supposed to happen but you know did not happen?

4.

Okay. Let me shift the focus.

6. What was the first thought you can recall having at the time it happened, or when you first found out about it?

7. As you think about it now, what one thought stands out the most in your mind?

8. Of all the thoughts you had, the things you did, or the reactions you experienced, which one thought or reaction are you most surprised you even had? (What surprised you the most about you?)

9. Was there anything you thought you wished you would have done or said differently?

10. Is there anything you did that left you second guessing yourself or not quite sure you handled as effectively as you could have with some preparation?

11. If something similar were to happen again how do you think you might react differently?

Thank you. At this point, I'm going to let _____ continue.

5.

Personal Reaction Stage

We are going to look at personal reactions now. Let me ask:

1. What was the worst moment for you?

2. Where did you feel the hurt or the fear the most in your body?

3. What scared you the most then?

4. What scares you now?

5. What reactions are you having that you might be afraid to let others know about because you think these reactions are not normal?

6.

6. What other reactions are you having that are new to you, persistent, seem strange, or are worrisome to you? Are there any traumatic dreams, flashbacks, intrusive thoughts, etc.?

7. What worries you now that did not worry you before?

8. Is there anything you think might have been done that wasn't done or was done that didn't need to be done?

9. How has this incident changed your view of your life right now? (How you look at yourself, others around you, your work enviornment...)

7.

Summary Stage

Well, we are now at the final stage (debriefer can refer to notes). I am going to turn it over to _____.

Let me first summarize the main issues that came up today.

1. Normalize the reactions they identified during the session. . . "The reactions you described are not at all unusual . . . feeling responsible, having dreams, being easily startled, wanting it to be over, (be sure to address shame as a common reaction), etc."

2. Prepare them for ongoing reactions by using the handout . . . "Do not be surprised if weeks, even months, from now you experience. . ."

3. Use the additional handout to encourage them to take very good care of themselves physically.

8.

4. Discuss the fact that current reactions may continue or new reactions may yet emerge. This is normal during the first four weeks or so. Encourage them to call for assistance if the reactions go beyond 4-8 weeks or are causing them to perform or function poorly. (**Important exception:** Reactions may extend beyond the four week acute stress period when a person is involved in disasters or other external events where physical reminders cannot be avoided. The same may occur when the details of an incident are kept alive in the media for an extended period of time. Such events often necessitate follow-up debriefing sessions and extend recovery time.)

5. Ask: "Do you have any final questions?" Also ask: "What at this point in time might help you get through the next several days?"

<u>NOTE</u>: If such suggestions are forthcoming or problems related to management arise, <u>ask</u> if you might have a minute before they leave to talk with the administrator. Have the administrator sit with them briefly to decide what things can be done immediately and what will take more time to implement. **Do this following your closure.**

9.

6. **(Closure)** Thank you very much . . . I know how difficult it can be to revisit such a traumatic incident, but I think you'll find this will be helpful to you. You have our phone numbers. Please call anytime. (If you know you will be returning in four weeks for a follow up session, notify the group)

* Mingle for a few minutes after to answer personal questions and/or discreetly recommend to a participant that additional assistance might be helpful.

* Remember: Do not get into your car and drive away immediately. Wait at least 15 minutes before leaving. Talk with the other debriefers, take a short walk, and take some deep breaths before starting back home.

10.

When to Call for Help

Should you experience any of these reactions beyond the initial four week period following the incident, please call us immediately.

The traumatic event is persistently reexperienced in at least one of the following ways:

1. Recurrent and intrusive distressing recollections of the event, including images, thoughts, other memories of the incident..

2. Recurrent distressing dreams (nightmares) of the incident itself or any dream content that is terrifying.

3. Acting or feeling as if the traumatic event were recurring (includes a sense of reliving the experience).

4. Intense psychological distress at exposure to internal reminders that symbolize or resemble an aspect of the traumatic event. (Fear, anxiety and anger are possible examples.)

5. Physiological reactivity upon exposure to internal or external reminder that symbolize or resemble an aspect of the traumatic event. (Nausea, difficulty breathing, startle reaction and faintness are a few examples.)

Numbing and Avoidance

Persistent avoidance of reminders associated with the trauma or numbing of your feelings or responsiveness to others.

1. Efforts to avoid thoughts, feelings, or conversations associated with the trauma.

2. Efforts to avoid activities, places, or people that trigger memories of the trauma.

3. Inability to recall an important aspect of the trauma.

4. Markedly diminished interest or participation in significant activities often those having some association with the trauma.

5. Feeling of detachment or estrangement from others.

6. Restricted range of emotion (e.g., unable to have loving feelings).

7. Sense of a foreshortened future (e.g., do not expect to have a career, marriage, children, or a normal life span: cannot even think about a few days in advance).

Hyperarousal and Persistent Symptoms of Increased Arousal
(not present before the trauma - see note)

1. Difficulty falling or staying asleep

2. Irritability or outbursts of anger

3. Difficulty concentrating

4. Hypervigilance/ constant worry about something else happening

5. Exaggerated startle response (responses to sounds, smells, images, sights, tough that reminds you of what happened)

These reactions are not at all unusual during the first four weeks following a traumatic event. When involved in disasters or other external events in which physical reminders cannot be avoided and/or various aspects of the incident are kept alive such as in the case of media coverage, reactions may extend beyond the four week acute stress period.

Should any of these symptoms persist beyond a 4-8 week period and/or emerge as delayed reactions months later, we strongly recommend consultation with a trauma consultant.

NOTE: Trauma can induce biological and neurological changes which play a part in the ability to sleep, levels of anxiety, concentration, and other trauma-specific reactions. Should reactions persist beyond the four week period, consultation for temporary medication should be considered. The loss of sleep, intrusive thoughts, anxiety, and other reactions induced by trauma can deplete an individual of much needed physical rest and inner emotional calmness and precipitate yet more problems for the individual. Medication, at times, is simply a necessity. However, medication should only be temporary.

(gathered from the APA-DSM-IV)

You may contact us at _____.

Helpful Strategies For Trauma Victims/Survivors

- It is very important to your recovery to get enough rest, especially the first 4 - 6 weeks following the trauma.

    - If you cannot sleep at night, take "cat" naps of 15 minutes - 1/2 hour during the day.

    - If waking up during the night because of traumatic dreams know they will pass in time. Do what comforts you. Read a good book until you become sleepy again. Snack, watch television, listen to music, write, do some housework. Remember, this will be a temporary change.

- Exercise of some kind is important to help relieve you of the tension that traumatic experiences create. Even if you have not been exercising, go for a short walk. Walk the dog an extra time. Do housework or add a few minutes to your usual exercise routine.

- Avoid too much caffeine, alcohol, as they can stimulate your already over aroused brian or can intensify your emotions. Do not self medicate. NOTE: If you are having difficulties with relaxing or sleeping following the trauma, then call for a temporary prescription to help you sleep but if this persists beyond 4-6 weeks consult with a trauma specialist immediately.

- Pull back on making a commitment to additional responsibilities for the first four weeks. The tendency for some is to take on additional responsibilities thinking it will help them forget. In reality, it frequently drains them of energy, delays the healing process and intensifies future reactions when they finally emerge.

- Be protective and nurturing of yourself. It's okay to want to be by yourself, or just stay around home with the family. Eat whatever your comfort foods are, as frequently as you need. Let family, friends know that they can best help by taking care of themselves over the next several days while you do what helps you feel a bit better.

- Expect during the 4 - 6 weeks following the event that new memories of and reactions to your experience are likely to emerge. This does not mean things are getting worse. It takes time to heal.

- Understand that your trauma reactions need to be expressed and experienced by you in order for you to heal. Kids, for example, go to the same horror movie, like

Nightmare On Elm Street, four, five, six times, so they can master their fear, the terror they experience when seeing the movie for the first time.

- If any trauma reaction continues beyond six to eight weeks from when the trauma occurred, you really do need to talk with a trauma consultant. If you do not, such reactions can become chronic as well as create additional problems for you.

- We all have different reactions. What scares you may not scare someone else. If you are experiencing reactions after the six week period, it does not mean something is terribly wrong with you. It means your past experiences are such that you just don't know how to respond to what happened. Generally, talking to a trauma specialist a few times will resolve the problem.

- A traumatic experience can, however, terrorize the strongest and healthiest. It can induce such terror that our lives become disorganized or disoriented. We become someone strange or act in ways we have never acted before. This can panic us.

- Trauma is not an experience we want to keep to ourselves. It is, in fact, an experience we want to resolve as quickly as possible. Do not hesitate to consult with a trauma specialist when your reactions are overwhelming or interfere with normal functioning. The specialist can help you sort out which reactions are normal and can help you prepare for possible future reactions.

- Finally, traumatic experiences tend to change the way we look at life, our behaviors, activities, relationships and our future. Expect in the weeks to come to see the world differently, your friends, loved ones, work relationships. In time, you will redefine what you want for yourself.

- The first 4 - 6 weeks therefore is not a time to be making any major decisions. Put what you can on hold. During recovery from a trauma everything is a bit distorted. You want to wait whenever possible to deal with major decisions until after you have had time (4 - 6 weeks) to reorder your life and feel stable once again.

- Should you need further assistance call The National Institute for Trauma and Loss in Children (TLC) at (877) 306-5256.

Debriefing Teams Model
&
Individual Debriefing Format

This model is designed only for use with school crisis team members or agency staff who have been frontline responders. It can include a maximum of ten members. Some may be members of the local school crisis team and others from the district-wide team who assisted local school members during their crisis. It is also designed for use with those intervenors who have intervened with agency staff and clients. One or two consultants are needed to debrief debriefers. It is somewhat like group supervision, but more structured and focused.

This model is more flexible than the formal debriefing. Its purposes are: 1) to identify procedural or systemic issues of the school/agency which positively or negatively impacted efforts to support staff, students or clients, 2) to help debriefers process difficult personal reactions, and 3) to evaluate each debriefer's performance and the overall team performance.

One or two consultants are needed to debrief. If two consultants are used, they should work together while moving through the steps. Both can provide summaries and recommendations.

TIME NEEDED

Completing the "debriefing" of teams takes one - two hours.

STAGES

This process has four stages: System Issues, Personal Reactions, Individual and Team Performance, Summary and Recommendations.

GROUND RULES

The same rules used for debriefing apply to this process.

NOTE: This process greatly illustrates for teams what their experience(s) has taught them regarding their school's response, administrative strengths and weaknesses and each memeber's personal abilities. *In addition, we now recommend that the team, 2-3 weeks after the crisis, be taken through the formal debriefing to better ensure that personal reactions are addressed as well as delayed reactions/issues, which often emerge after the routine of daily life returns.*

111

Stage One - Procedural Systemic Issues

One consultant begins the session by identifying the three purposes of the process. He then explains that questions will be raised to explore and clarify what was done. At the end, summaries and recommendations will be provided.

NOTE: For your convenience the following questions are laid out so you can copy them and cut and paste them on 5" x 8" index cards. It may make it easier to use in this form.

Stage One - Procedural Systemic Issues

1. What surprised you most about the school/agency response to the incident?
2. Of the responses identified, which leave you with additional questions. What are those questions?
3. From where or from whom did you receive your strongest support for carrying out your tasks?
4. From where or from whom did you receive your greatest resistance?
5. What would you recommend that the system do differently to more effectively respond to future traumas?
6. What would you recommend be repeated?
7. What additional information or resources would have been helpful?

1.

Stage Two - Personal Reactions

1. What is the most difficult emotionally for you during the day, or evenings, when you are alone?
2. What were you not prepared for?
3. What was the worst part/moment for you?
4. On a scale of one to five, with five being "the most emotional intervention" you have conducted, how would you rate this situation? (If this is your first intervention? Use the same scale to identify the level of emotional intensity for you - five being the most intense)
4. What specific details or situations stands out most in your mind at this time?
5. As you think about it now, what one thought stands out the most for you?
6. Of all the reactions you had (cognitively and/or emotionally), or things you did, what reactions are you surprised you that you even had, or what surprised you about yourself and your reactions?

2.

Stage Three - Individual and Team Evaluation

1. As a team, on a scale of one to five with five being very good, how would you rate your cohesiveness and comfort level with one another? Provide an example to support your rating.
2. On a scale of one to five with five being the highest value, how would you rate the effectiveness of your intervention? Explain the reason for your rating.
3. What, if anything, would you have done differently as a team?
4. If you were a supervisor, what one suggestion would you make to your team to enhance, reinforce, prepare it for future interventions?
5. If asked to evaluate your own performance, what one recommendation/suggestion would you present yourself?

3.

Stage Four – Summary and Recommendations

This is an opportunity for debriefing consultants to teach, reinforce, and enhance intervenor's skills and insights. It is important to be honest with observations and recommendations.

1. Begin with observations related to school/agency procedural and systemic issues and the recommendations you would suggest presently to the appropriate person(s). This is a place were some teaching related to system issues may be appropriate. Ask participants if they have additional comments or thoughts to add before moving on.
2. Normalize personal reactions shared by participants. It will help to understand some of the countertransference issues (vicarious traumatization) all are vulnerable to experiencing. If needed, different perceptions can be provided. If there is a significantly difficult personal issue, consider waiting to address it until you can discuss it privately with that individual. Stress the importance of self care as needed at this time.
3. A good closure point is to comment on the overall group interactions and the issues to consider for future interventions. Make yourself available for a brief time following the session should one of the participants want to discuss things further. Do let them know how you can be reached if they have additional questions or concerns.

4.

Self Debriefing

Should access to debriefing not be available it will be important for you to move through the following questions designed to help you partially "debrief" until you can go through the more formal process. This will help to:

1) Identify and correct problem areas

2) Prepare for subsequent sessions and potential problem areas

3) Identify personal sources of anxiety and determine strategies to minimize them

4) Eliminate second guessing your responses to children

5) Minimize stress brought about by the always difficult references to death and trauma

Move through each debriefing question in the order presented:

1) What were your first thoughts about the incident?

2) Of the thoughts you had, what one thought surprised you most?

3) What was the worst moment for you e.g., activity, child's response, your response?

4) Was your response to this difficult moment appropriate at the time? If you felt it was not, why not? What would you do differently?

5) What was the most surprising moment of any of the interventions provided e.g., child's response, behavior?

6) What factors made it surprising to you e.g., what was said, done, not done?

7) What did this incident make you aware of about your own personal experience, feelings, attitudes? What did it make you aware of about your own professional knowledge and skills?

8) What wouldn't you do again in a similar situation?

9) What would you do differently or the same in a similar situation?

10) What was the most rewarding aspect of the interventions provided?

11) What do you need to do to prepare for the next incident?

12) What do you need to do to take care of yourself during your personal time today?

NOTE: It will be helpful to write down your responses in a notebook, then review and compare them with your next debriefing responses. You may be surprised by patterns that emerge as well as by your own insights.

Appendix F
Defusing Model

The formal defusing model is intended to be used 3-4 days following exposure. It, too, is intended only for the most-exposed. However, some younger children may need more attention sooner than the 3-4 day guideline.

We suggest *Helping Children Feel Safe* as a resource for activities to initiate in the first few days. It is designed to help restore their sense of safety.

It is important to appreciate that you will need to be flexible with your interventions with younger children. Keep parents informed and, if you are moving children into this formal defusing, it must be with parental consent. "Group" children by appropriate ages and developmental stages. For example, do not mix 6-year-olds with 10-year-olds. Furthermore, do not place witnesses in the same group as non-witnesses. Exposure to witness detail may induce unnecessary anxiety and arousal. Should you not be able to separate these two groups DO NOT ask questions about details. Follow the "non-witness" questions presented in this model.

PLEASE NOTE: The formal debridfing model is very cognitive in its process. Younger children 1st through 6th grade have a more limite cognitive ability than adolescents and, therefore, be unable to participate in the formal model. Defusing is the TLC Model which limits cognitive processes and focuses more on sensory activities to help them find relief from the neurophysiological experiences of fear, terror and feeling unsafe. At their age it is difficult to put these body sensations in any cognitive contextual framework, therefore the need for sensory activities directed at releasing the sensory outcomes of trauma eposure. The emotional sensory arousal their bodies now experience cannot be altered through cognitive processes alone (Levine and Kline, 2008; van der Kolk, 2006; LeDeux, 2000).

Defusing Model

The TLC Defusing Model relies on a brief cognitive process followed by sensory activities which give younger children the opportunity to tell of the details of their experience in a medium they feel safe using. Drawing and story telling aided by trauma-specific questions, provide both the medium and focus needed to help them find relief from the terror of their experience.

The Defusing Model again is only for the most exposed and to be used 3-4 days following the incident with those who are still struggling after your efforts at crisis intervention and use sensory activities (*Helping Children Feel Safe*).

<u>Stages</u>
Introduction, Generalization, Specification, Externalization, Summary

The examples used are to provide a framework. Use those words and examples, which are age appropriate, but also cover the themes presented in this outline.

<u>**NOTE**</u>: Have their teacher present if possible or another familiar staff person to help ease their fear and even doubts about you as stranger. When working with younger children, flexibility is critical. Keep in mind that you may need to meet with some younger children several times because their exposure has triggered numerous issues. *Helping Children Feel Safe* activities can be used immediately with the younger children to help minimize the need for additional debriefing. They can also be used after the formal defusing process if determined they would be helpful.

Introduction

This time is to explain to children who you are, why you are there, and what you will be doing, what they will be doing, and how they will be asked to do it (ground rules). Be brief.

Hello, our names are _____ and _____. We are here because of ___(event)___. When these kinds of things happen to us and people we know, all kinds of new feelings and thoughts can also happen inside us, which never happened before. Maybe we have bad dreams or feel sad. Maybe we feel mad or afraid, or we just don't want to think about what happened. You probably have questions about what happened, too.

We have met with other children who had the same kind of thing happen as your school/or special group. They talked with us about what happened, drew pictures and helped us understand how things like this made them think and feel. They told us they felt much better and not so scared afterwards.

We want to know what this has been like for you.

First, we are going to ask you to follow these simple rules:

• When you want to say something or ask something, raise your hand just like you do for your teacher or group leader.

• When one of you is talking, all of us will listen. No one else will start talking or interrupt.

• It is okay in here to be sad, cry, be afraid, and talk about what happened. Talking will help all of us feel better. It is also okay not to talk. It is not okay to make fun of anyone who is sad, scared or cries. Even _____ and I are sad about what happened.

Add additional rules if deemed necessary, but keep to a minimum. You can add rules related to activities when you get to that stage.

Generalization

At this point you are to provide a generalized definition and/or description of the nature of the incident followed by questions as to previous experiences the children may have had with 1) the type of incident that occurred (accident), 2) generalized nature of the incident (violent) or 3) generalized reactions it may have created (really scary).

Example 1: (Accident) What happened to Mrs. Jones was an accident. Accidents do not always kill people. People do not always die from accidents. Some accidents hurt really bad and other accidents are real small and don't hurt much at all. Some accidents are as small as falling off our bikes or spilling our milk, and others are really big like when a home catches fire and burns down or when someone is in a car and gets hit by another car. Sometimes accidents just happen. It is nobody's fault. Sometimes people aren't careful or paying attention and cause accidents to happen. We can't tell when an accident is going to happen, it just happens real quick.   (Words will change depending upon age level of children)

How many of you have had a small or big accident? (Ask for their examples)

"Other than what happened to _(incident)_ how many know someone who has had a bad accident?" (Ask for their examples).

NOTE: It is far easier for children to initially talk and respond to questions about similar types of situations than to begin talking immediately about the recent trauma. As they answer just a few of your questions in the initial stage, it helps to release the tension and makes it much easier for them to move directly to talking and asking questions about the specific incident.

Another example for using generalized nature of incident.

Example 2: (Murder is violent in nature) What happened to _____ was very violent. Violence is what happens when someone gets so mad or so upset they don't care who they hurt or even kill.

Violent people don't always kill people, sometimes they just hurt them real bad. Sometimes mean people yell and scream and call people bad names and make them feel really bad. It's okay to get mad sometimes isn't it? But it is not okay to be violent and call people bad names or try to hurt people, is it?

In the last week what is the most violent thing you have seen on television or at the movies? (Ask for their examples). How many of you know of someone who

had something very violent happen to them? (Ask for their examples).
Example 3: (Reaction; example is fear.) "What happened to __(incident)__ what happened yesterday when __(incident)__ was very scary. Sometimes when scary things happen people get hurt really bad or sometimes people don't get hurt at all. Sometimes we stayed scared for a long time. Other than what happened ... what is the scariest thing that ever happened to you ... someone you know ... ?

(Ask for their examples)

Specification/Factual

Once children have shared their experience related to the generalized components of the incident move directly to the specific incident.

Now it is time to talk about __(incident)__. What have you been told happened? (Get their responses. There is no need to correct misperceptions, false information at this time. It will impede the process of externalization of their fantasies, fears, and reactions. Simply listen and acknowledge by eye contact. Correction of misinformation and fantasies can be done during summarization).

The phrasing of questions

Questions at this point will differ based upon their exposure. If they were actual witnesses questions will be directed to, "What did you see, hear, or remember happening? If they were not actual witnesses then questions will be directed to, "What do you might know or have you heard about what happened?" (Allow children to respond.)

Questions for Non-Witnesses:

Since this happened, what is your biggest worry?
What have you been told, or heard, about what happened?

Questions for Witnesses:

When this happened what did you see? What did you hear? What did you do? What happened to you? Did you know __victim(s)__ really well? What do you think most about with what happened? Since this happened, what is your biggest worry?

Personal

At this time you will be allowing an opportunity for children to express personal reactions. Not all children will have a response, that is healthy and is to be normalized by stating: "Not all of you may be ready to talk about what happened and that is okay."

Questions:
The purpose is to normalize their experience. A show of hands following questions works well.

How many of you have had bad, scary dreams since this happened?
During the day, how many of you see pictures of what happened in your mind?
During the day, how many of you think about the things that happened?

Normalize all their reactions/responses to these questions.

To ask additional questions within the group will make it far too cognitive. Depending upon age level some children may not have the words to describe their reactions and will not be able to do so unless provided an opportunity to use metaphors, which the next stage provides. In addition, you want to provide each child the opportunity to participate actively. Asking too many questions will prolong the duration of the process beyond a manageable and productive period.

Remember this is not group treatment, but simply an opportunity for them to communicate to us how they have been impacted by the trauma and for us to teach them that what they are experiencing is quite normal given their experience.

Externalization

NOTE: This model is designed as an initial, one-time defusing for young children. However, some children may need more assistance following this session. Depending upon age we recommend either *What Color Is Your Hurt?* (3-6 years old) or *I Feel Better Now!* (6-12 years old).

At this point you will be asking them to draw. Have 8 1/2" x 11" sheets of plain paper and either colored pencils or fine point markers available for everyone. Give each child one sheet of paper. A detailed step-by-step description of this process is found in *Structured Sensory Interventions for Traumatized Children, Adolescents and Parents* (Steele and Raider, 2001). This textbook is available through TLC, in addition to *Children of Trauma: Tools to Help the Helper*, a 50-minute video, which demonstrates this process on an individual basis.

Why is drawing effective?

Muteness, non-responsiveness, numbness and detachment are common reactions when interviewing traumatized children, adolescents or even adults. Malchiodi (2008),Steele and Raider (2001), Hafern and Peterson (1982), Pynoos (1986), and others concur that trauma produces such severe reactions that it often needs an indirect, yet focused response to overcome the inability to talk about what happened. Drawing provides this indirect approach, while your questions about their drawings provide the trauma focus.

Drawing:
- is a psychomotor activity that takes a person from the passive stance of a victim to the stance of a survivor
- provides a safe, non-threatening vehicle of communication to tell the details of the trauma
- provides a sense of control and empowerment; as drawings can be changed, erased, or thrown away
- provides a stimulus for storytelling

Instructions for this drawing activity:
1) I want you to draw a picture of what happened that you can then tell us a story about. You can draw whatever you like.

2) Follow this by giving each child an opportunity to tell the story about their drawing. (One to two minutes.)

3) If they have trouble telling their story, ask questions about the components of their drawing: each person in it, inanimate objects, what is happening, where they are in their drawing, what they are doing, and so on.

There is no need to offer reflections or normalize at this point. They are externalizing their experience by drawing and by telling their story, as brief or as long as it may be. Once it is "outside" them, it becomes more manageable and less frightening. The process allows movement from the passive stance of victim (helpless) to the active stance of survivor (taking control, participating in their own recovery). It also now makes you a visual witness to its impact on them.

Once each child has told his story, move to the final stage. If time permits, we suggest the *Worry Activity* (pages 125 & 126) also found in all TLC's intervention programs.

Final Stage
Summary

After each child has completed his story it is time to normalize all the reactions they have experienced - the fear, the hurt, the worry, the sadness, and the anger.

Example
- When something like this happens, you sometimes are afraid to go to sleep because you have terrible nightmares.

- Sometimes things like this make you worry that something bad will happen to you or someone you really love, even during the day.

- Sometimes it makes you really mad. You want to do something bad to the person who did this.

- Having nightmares, being worried and mad, is normal after a trauma.

- You are not alone. Some of you may have these reactions. It's okay. What happened was very . . .

RECOMMENDATION: Working with the younger children can be more difficult than working with adolescents and adults. Younger children do not have the words to describe what happened, are not able to understand as much, and are far more vulnerable because they must rely on the adult world to support them.

It is not always easy to find the words and ways to help younger children reestablish trust and a sense of safety, following the impact of a traumatic event. We strongly recommend reading *Brave Bart: A Story for Traumatized and Grieving Children*, the story of a kitten who is traumatized and helped to become a survivor by a neighborhood cat (Helping Hannah). It contains the metaphors, normalizations, labeling of feelings, and cognitive reframing needed to help younger children move from victim to survivor. *Brave Bart* is an excellent tool to use during the summary stage. It will make your efforts far more effective and will reinforce how courageous they have been in the face of terror.

You will probably want to return for a follow-up session with the group 4-6 weeks after the incident when additional issues can be addressed and you can better evaluate those children who are still struggling beyond the acute stress stage and in need of individual attention and/or trauma-specific group intervention.

Final Activity

It is important to follow up the summary stage with something fun. You can have refreshments, play a game, do a group mural. You choose.

We do not recommend sending drawings home as parents will not understand that the purpose of the drawing was not an artistic one but simply to give children the opportunity to make us a witness to their experience.

Worry Activity

The Worry Activity sheet is on page 126. Simply ask the children to identify their biggest worry and write their biggest worry on the activity sheet. You can do it for them if needed. Then, ask them to color in the box that shows how little or big their worry is at this time. When finished use the following reflections to help the children be less anxious about their worry.

Reflections:

• We all have worries. It is very normal to have worries when scary things happen.

• When it rains it doesn't rain forever, does it? NO. Worries don't last forever either.

• Some worries seem like there is nothing we can do to change or stop them.

• But we can't do anything to stop the rain either, but it stops, doesn't it? YES.

• And when it rains, don't we usually find something to do until it stops? Sure we do.

When we have a really big worry, there are things we can do until the worry goes away, too. What kind of things can we do? We can . . .

When finished, close by engaging the children in a fun activity, snacks

NOTE: A week or two later meet with the children and give them their worry pages, plus a new page. Have them rewrite their same worry on the new page, but now fill in how much *smaller* or bigger their worry is now. For many, it will be smaller. If it is as large further evaluation related to anxiety, fear etc. should be initiated.

My biggest worry is _____.

This is how big or little my worry is today:
Color the box that best shows how little or big your worry is today.

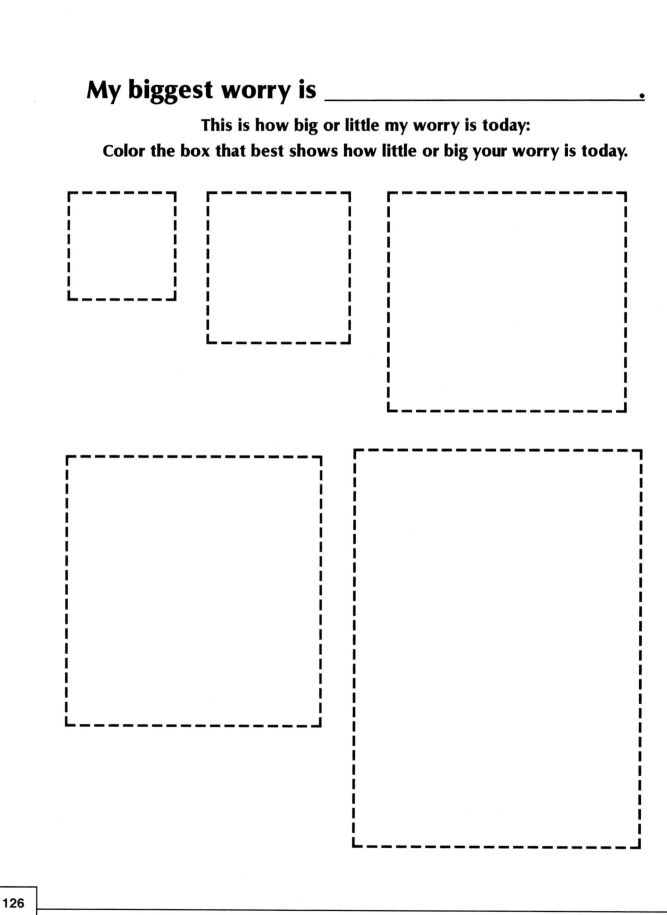

Appendix G
Operational Debriefing

Operational Debriefing
O D
(Review Chapter Nine for Process Instructions)

Group Size: Any number.

Group Membership: Schools - all staff.
Agencies - line staff separate from administrators/ managers/supervisors. Please note earlier discussion of differences generally found between school systems and agency systems where it is generally more beneficial to separate the line staff from administrative staff. Smaller agencies and/or administrators who insist on total staff participation at the same session are the exception.

When: End of first full or second day of incident with one follow up to be determined by the outcome of this initial meeting. It is generally beneficial to have an additional session three-five days later.

Duration: One hour.

NOTE: **Debriefers should be consultants from the community to minimize resistance and increase objectivity.**

Introduce this process by informing staff that the session will run no longer than one hour. Its purpose is to identify: 1) what has worked well and what has not; 2) current concerns and worries; 3) additional interventions which are still needed; 4) additional resources or assistance to make the next several days easier. Inform them you will be asking questions about students/clients, their own experiences, and procedural issues and then summarize your observations and comments. Begin with stage one.

Stage One - Student/Client Reactions

1. What behaviors of students/clients were most upsetting for you?

2. What were you not prepared to see or hear from students/clients?

3. What worries you the most about students/clients?

4. What happened with students/clients that didn't need to happen?

5. What didn't happen that should have happened or still needs to happen?

Stage Two - Staff Reactions

1. What one thought stands out the most in your mind about anything you saw or heard?

2. Of all the thoughts, emotional reactions, and things you've done during this crisis, what surprises you the most. (This question is not what surprised them about other's actions/reactions but their own thoughts, emotions. Keep them focused on their reactions).

3. What behaviors among other staff surprised you the most?

4. What has been the worst part for you?

5. Where have you felt the impact most in your body?

6. What additional physical reactions have some of you been experiencing?

7. If you were to go through this again, what would you do differently?

Stage Three - Administrative Issues

1. What still needs to happen, either immediately or over the next several days, to help you out?

2. Are there any unanswered questions or additional information you need?

3. What have been some of the positive things that have happened?

(Questions 2 and 3 can be partially answered by administrative staff, if present)

129

Stage Four -

1. Similar to debriefing, this is the place for you to **educate staff about trauma reactions, what they might experience in the following days and, ways to care for themselves**, etc.

2. It is important not only to normalize the reactions they have experienced but also to **normalize the system response**, especially if this is the first critical incident experienced. It is essential to **be honest regarding the need for additional training**, and improvements needed on their crisis plan, policies and procedures. An honest appraisal now will help them be better prepared in the future. It is also important to stress the strength that has emerged, the dedicated caring, etc.

3. It is also **appropriate to ask if they have any questions of you** and they often will. Questions generally refer to your experiences with other systems and how they managed in comparison. Inform them that you will be having a detailed consultation with the principal, superintendent, executive director, etc. about their recommendations and your own. It is appropriate to mention what some of your recommendations may be if you know at the time.

    Notify them that you will be available for a few minutes should they have personal questions or comments to share with you.

    Provide them with encouragement and affirmations for their care and concern and dedication to students/clients. Thank them. Remind them that if they do have concerns about specific individuals to see one of the crisis team members (debriefers) immediately following this meeting.

    Your responsibility does include a consultation with the appropriate sources related to your observations and recommendations. This can be done following the OD session and followed if needed with a written report (general).

    Pass out materials prior to this session as you may want to reference them during your presentation.

When to Call for Help

Should you experience any of these reactions beyond the initial four week period following the incident, please call us immediately.

The traumatic event is persistently reexperienced in at least one of the following ways:

1. Recurrent and intrusive distressing recollections of the event, including images, thoughts, other memories of the incident..

2. Recurrent distressing dreams (nightmares) of the incident itself or any dream content that is terrifying.

3. Acting or feeling as if the traumatic event were recurring (includes a sense of reliving the experience).

4. Intense psychological distress at exposure to internal reminders that symbolize or resemble an aspect of the traumatic event. (Fear, anxiety and anger are possible examples.)

5. Physiological reactivity upon exposure to internal or external reminders that symbolize or resemble an aspect of the traumatic event. (Nausea, difficulty breathing, startle reaction and faintness are a few examples.)

Numbing and Avoidance

Persistent avoidance of reminders associated with the trauma or numbing of your feelings or responsiveness to others.

1. Efforts to avoid thoughts, feelings, or conversations associated with the trauma.

2. Efforts to avoid activities, places, or people that trigger memories of the trauma.

3. Inability to recall an important aspect of the trauma.

4. Markedly diminished interest or participation in significant activities, often those having some association with the trauma.

5. Feeling of detachment or estrangement from others.

6. Restricted range of emotion (e.g., unable to have loving feelings).

7. Sense of a foreshortened future (e.g., do not expect to have a career, marriage, children, or a normal life span: cannot even think about a few days in advance).

Hyperarousal and Persistent Symptoms of Increased Arousal
(not present before the trauma - see note)

1. Difficulty falling or staying asleep

2. Irritability or outbursts of anger

3. Difficulty concentrating

4. Hypervigilance/ constant worry about something else happening

5. Exaggerated startle response (responses to sounds, smells, images, sights, tough that reminds you of what happened)

These reactions are not at all unusual during the first four weeks following a traumatic event. When involved in disasters or other external events in which physical reminders cannot be avoided and/or various aspects of the incident are kept alive such as in the case of media coverage, reactions may extend beyond the four week acute stress period.

Should any of these symptoms persist beyond a 4-8 week period and/or emerge as delayed reactions months later, we strongly recommend consultation with a trauma consultant.

NOTE: Trauma can induce biological and neurological changes which play a part in the ability to sleep, levels of anxiety, concentration, and other trauma-specific reactions. Should reactions persist beyond the four week period, consultation for temporary medication should be considered. The loss of sleep, intrusive thoughts, anxiety, and other reactions induced by trauma can deplete an individual of much needed physical rest and inner emotional calmness and precipitate yet more problems for the individual. Medication, at times, is simply a necessity. However, medication should only be temporary.

(gathered from the APA-DSM-IV)

Helpful Strategies For Trauma Victims/Survivors

- It is very important to your recovery to get enough rest, especially the first 4 - 6 weeks following the trauma.

    - If you cannot sleep at night, take "cat" naps of 15 minutes - 1/2 hour during the day.

    - If waking up during the night because of traumatic dreams know they will pass in time. Do what comforts you. Read a good book until you become sleepy again. Snack, watch television, listen to music, write, do some housework. Remember, this will be a temporary change.

- Exercise of some kind is important to help relieve you of the tension that traumatic experiences create. Even if you have not been exercising, go for a short walk. Walk the dog an extra time. Do housework or add a few minutes to your usual exercise routine.

- Avoid too much caffeine, alcohol, as they can stimulate your already over aroused brian or can intensify your emotions. Do not self medicate. <u>NOTE</u>: If you are having difficulties with relaxing or sleeping following the trauma, then call for a temporary prescription to help you sleep but if this persists beyond 4-6 weeks consult with a trauma specialist immediately.

- Pull back on making a commitment to additional responsibilities for the first four weeks. The tendency for some is to take on additional responsibilities thinking it will help them forget. In reality, it frequently drains them of energy, delays the healing process and intensifies future reactions when they finally emerge.

- Be protective and nurturing of yourself. It's okay to want to be by yourself, or just stay around home with the family. Eat whatever your comfort foods are, as frequently as you need. Let family, friends know that they can best help by taking care of themselves over the next several days while you do what helps you feel a bit better.

- Expect during the 4 - 6 weeks following the event that new memories of and reactions to your experience are likely to emerge. This does not mean things are getting worse. It takes time to heal.

- Understand that your trauma reactions need to be expressed and experienced by

133

you in order for you to heal. Kids, for example, go to the same horror movie, like *Nightmare On Elm Street*, four, five, six times, so they can master their fear, the terror they experience when seeing the movie for the first time.

- If any trauma reaction continues beyond six to eight weeks from when the trauma occurred, you really do need to talk with a trauma consultant. If you do not, such reactions can become chronic as well as create additional problems for you.

- We all have different reactions. What scares you may not scare someone else. If you are experiencing reactions after the six week period, it does not mean something is terribly wrong with you. It means your past experiences are such that you just don't know how to respond to what happened. Generally, talking to a trauma specialist a few times will resolve the problem.

- A traumatic experience can, however, terrorize the strongest and healthiest. It can induce such terror that our lives become disorganized or disoriented. We become someone strange or act in ways we have never acted before. This can panic us.

- Trauma is not an experience we want to keep to ourselves. It is, in fact, an experience we want to resolve as quickly as possible. Do not hesitate to consult with a trauma specialist when your reactions are overwhelming or interfere with normal functioning. The specialist can help you sort out which reactions are normal and can help you prepare for possible future reactions.

- Finally, traumatic experiences tend to change the way we look at life, our behaviors, activities, relationships and our future. Expect in the weeks to come to see the world differently, your friends, loved ones, work relationships. In time, you will redefine what you want for yourself.

- The first 4 - 6 weeks therefore is not a time to be making any major decisions. Put what you can on hold. During recovery from a trauma everything is a bit distorted. You want to wait whenever possible to deal with major decisions until after you have had time (4 - 6 weeks) to reorder your life and feel stable once again.

- Should you need further assistance call The National Institute for Trauma and Loss in Children (TLC) at (877) 306-5256.

PTSD Reactions in Children

* <u>Cognitive dysfunction</u> involving memory and learning. "A" students become "C" students; severe reactions cause others to fail altogether.

* <u>Inability to concentrate</u>. Children who once could complete two and three different tasks now have difficulty with a single task. Parents and educators often react negatively to this behavior because they simply do not understand the "why" that causes it.

* <u>Tremendous fear and anxiety</u>. One 17 month old boy who witnessed his father kill his mother is now 7 years old. He still sleeps on the floor, ever ready to run from danger. Six year old Elizabeth, whose sister was killed one year earlier, is also sleeping on the floor. She did not witness her sister's murder, yet she is experiencing this same hypervigilant PTSD response.

Increased aggression, fighting, assaultive behavior - these are the first reactions generally identified as a change since the trauma. Revenge is a constant theme when the incident has been a violent one. Other reactions may include:

* <u>Survivor guilt</u>: Students not in school at the time of a random shooting and subsequent death of a fellow student may feel accountable and experience intrusive thoughts and images. Another form of survivor guilt is the belief that "It should have been me instead" or "I wish it would have been me instead."

* <u>Intrusive images (flashbacks)</u>: Two years later, teachers still notice this teenage girl engaging in a plucking motion with her hand. She was home when the beating occurred. She did not know her mother was already dead when she ran to help her. When she rolled her mother over, her mother's mouth was filled with blood and broken teeth. The daughter began pulling the broken teeth from her mother's mouth so she wouldn't choke on them. Two years later, that plucking motion still occurs when she's reexperiencing her experience.

* <u>Traumatic dreams</u>: 11 year old Tommy was a survivor, not a witness, when we first met him one year after his sister was killed by a serial killer. He was still having dreams of his "guts" being ripped out by Candyman. His sister had been stabbed repeatedly in the chest/stomach area.

* <u>Inappropriate age-related behavior</u>: These include clinging to mother, enuresis, and other regressive behaviors. Eleven year old Tommy, the boy mentioned above, has started to stutter.

* <u>Startle reactions</u>: After her father beat her mother to death, the police arrived to take pictures and arrest the father. Two years later, this daughter still cannot allow her picture to be taken because it reminds her of that day.

* <u>Emotional detachment</u>: Fifteen year old Mary, whose sister was also killed by a serial killer, had made friends her mother described as "real trouble". She never even cried at the funeral. She had received help but not the trauma-specific help we provided her.

Behaviorally, children may exhibit the following:

* Trouble sleeping, being afraid to sleep alone even for short periods of time.

* Be easily startled (terrorized) by sounds, sights, smells similar to those that existed at the time of the event - a car backfiring may sound like the gun shot that killed someone; for one child, his dog pouncing down the stairs brought back the sound of his father falling down the stairs and dying.

* Become hypervigilant - forever watching out for and anticipating that they are about to be or are in danger.

* Seek safety "spots" in their environment, in whatever room they may be in at the time. Children who sleep on the floor instead of their bed after a trauma do so because they fear the comfort of a bed will let them sleep so hard that they won't hear danger coming.

* Become irritable, aggressive, act tough, provoke fights.

* Verbalize a desire for revenge.

* Act as if they are no longer afraid of anything or anyone, verbalizing that nothing ever scares them anymore and in the face of danger, respond inappropriately.

* Forget recently acquired skills.

* Return to behaviors they had previously stopped, i.e. bed wetting, nail biting, or developing disturbing behaviors such as stuttering.

* Withdraw and want to do less with their friends.

* Develop headaches, stomach problems, fatigue, and other ailments not previously present.

* Becoming accident prone, taking risks they had previously avoided, putting themselves in life threatening situations, reenacting the event as a victim or a hero.

* Developing a pessimistic view of the future, losing their resilience to overcome additional difficulties, losing hope, losing their passion to survive, play, and enjoy life.

Adults may express Acute Stress/PTSD with the following behaviors (Johnson, 1993):

* Seems disconnected/preoccupied
* Not as neat in dress and habits
* Late, many absences, fatigued
* Low morale, change of attitude toward work
* Avoids certain situations/places
* Talks compulsively or not at all about incident
* Irritable, conflicts with others, and possibly with you
* Drinking, drug use
* Sudden change in lifestyle
* Aches, pains, illnesses
* Unhappiness, dissatisfaction

Lenore Terr (1991) makes a distinction between Type I and Type II traumas. Type I trauma refers to those incidents which are short-term and unexpected. Usually these are one time incidents of limited duration and could include rape, natural disasters, car accidents, etc.

Type II traumas are sustained and repeated exposure to a series of events or exposure to a single prolonged event. Repeated abuse, is an example of singular, prolonged, but repeated exposure. Type II traumas frequently lead to long-term interpersonal and characterological problems or to complex PTSD reactions when left untreated.

Trauma Debriefing: Structuring Larger Groups

by
William Steele, MSW, PsyD and Tricia Trimble, MEd, LPC, CTS

At times, traumatic incidents occur that involve a large number of people who could benefit from debriefing in small groups of eight to ten participants, but situations only allow for meeting in larger numbers of twenty to thirty plus participants at one time. Obviously, the debriefing process must be adjusted to accommodate the larger numbers (Steele W. and Trimble, T. 2001).

Trauma specialists may only be provided with one opportunity to meet with this large group. It is our belief that you cannot properly debrief more than eight people in a group setting, as it takes close to two hours for all participants to have the opportunity to tell their stories. Also, we do not encourage debriefing to go past two hours because of the risk of participants becoming overwhelmed and too exhausted to protect their emotional "self." So, what can trauma specialists do?

The National Institute has learned over the past eleven years that some intervention is better than no intervention for trauma victims. We have, in the past, often been asked to debrief groups of twenty or more professionals. We will provide two examples and discuss how they were approached. One group (Group A) consisted of teachers, social workers, counselors, and administrators in a school setting combined with mental health professionals called in to assist school personnel. The other group (Group B) was made up of law enforcement personnel. Both situations involved a shooting death; the one of a student inside the school, the other of an officer in the community.

Most vs. Least Exposed

When first called, we were informed that there were approximately twenty to thirty participants who wanted us to meet with them, including those who were at the scene during the traumatic incident and therefore, most exposed at the visual and the sensory level. Attempts to persuade (educate) the administrators to allow us to debrief no more than eight participants in multiple sessions, conducted simultaneously, failed. Efforts to initially meet with the most exposed separately, apart from the others also failed. This necessitated the "rescripting" of the debriefing process, especially the opening statements.

Structuring Opening Statements

In the larger format, it is very important to immediately readjust expectations of the group as to what can be accomplished in a large group. It is also important to say that additional help may be needed because the group size prohibits you from addressing all the questions used in a formal debriefing.

After introducing yourselves to the group, briefly mention that experience has taught you that debriefing can be helpful and can accelerate the healing process. Follow this brief opening with the following structuring statements:

"Debriefing is usually conducted with no more that eight persons in a group to give each person an opportunity to tell their complete story, their thoughts, the ways the situation has impacted them. This is not possible with your group so we have selected just a few questions of the many we normally ask. Because this will be an abbreviated debriefing, some of you may want an additional session to give yourselves the opportunity to get relief from some of the issues we may not be able to address today.

"There are, as you know, those of you here today who were on the scene when _____ happened or there immediately after, and those who were there much later and therefore, not exposed to the same elements. Those of you who were there please feel free not to answer our questions. It is perfectly okay, especially in a large group like this. Not everyone will have a lot to say or much to say today, but listening to your colleagues and peers will be helpful to you."

Order

Group A (teachers, social workers, counselors, and administrators along with mental health professionals) was directed to raise their hands if they wished to respond to the question posed above. A final check was made before going on to the next question to see if anyone wished to add anything. A visual scan should be made from one end of the semi circle to the other end in order to make sure that all participants have acknowledged the questions. In Group B, the law enforcement group, those on the scene were asked to respond first followed by other participants in a sequential order that was then continued. Both methods worked well. Ms. Trimble, one of the debriefers of the law enforcement group, was familiar with the team members, but the only member not in law enforcement. Only three of the twenty some participants in Group A were familiar to Dr. Steele. Confidentiality and other ground rules were established at this point.

Gaining Credibility

Ms. Trimble was introduced by an officer in Group B who was on the debriefing team. Because other team members had not previously conducted a debriefing, they asked Ms. Trimble to start the process. Knowing that law enforcement and other "first responders" often feel out of control and helpless, especially when one of their own has died, she took a few minutes to address how these reactions could leave them not wanting to talk. She also acknowledged that they might be cautious about what they did say, because this process was new to them and, because she herself was not in law enforcement. She then indicated that the process is generally very helpful, and that they would benefit in some way. Following this she thanked them for allowing her " in" to help.

Dr. Steele initiated similar comments with Group A and especially directed his attention to the concern that school personnel might have with responding in a group with non-school personnel. The same applied to non-school personnel. He invited participants to call him anytime should there be things they would like to talk or ask about following the debriefing.

Debriefers of both groups found that participants were appreciative of their honesty, sensitivity to these issues, and directness. Many reported afterward that they needed to hear these comments from the debriefers in order to feel comfortable with participating.

Questions

Both group debriefings took place approximately one week after the incident, after the victim's funeral. Debriefers of both groups began by first asking who the participants were and their relationship to the victim. This gave each participant the opportunity to respond regardless of the nature of their exposure. "Where were you when it happened, or when you first found out, and what did you do?" was the next question. This led to participants identifying different details related to varied aspects of the events that followed that day and that week. The one question not asked in both groups was, "What do you remember seeing and hearing?" There was concern that if those who were witnesses went into too much detail as to what they saw (the sensory), that it might make it more difficult for the non-witnesses to process their existing reactions.

The next question asked was, "What one thought stands out the most for you since this happened?" In both cases participants talked about their own reactions to different parts of all that happened. The issues of "should haves" or "I could haves" at the funeral and, even having to be in the group, were some of the issues that emerged. These questions, in both situations, set the stage for those who were initially reluctant to participate (reported by participants before leaving). It made it far easier for them to respond later.

When asked, "What was the worst part?" both group participants identified events following the incident such as the funeral, the media issues, community members, parent reactions; specific factors reminding them of what happened and difficulties they experienced in trying to help the most exposed. Personal reactions as well as system issues were discussed.

When asked, "Of all the thoughts or reactions you had, what one reaction or thought surprised you the most?" participants detailed more personal reactions, e.g. disbelief, denial, not being able to think clearly, being numb, confused, moving in slow motion, freezing, and not able to perform simple tasks such as dialing frequently called phone numbers. In the law enforcement group (Group B), those who apprehended the killer of the officer some seven hours later talked about being surprised at their being able to properly treat the killer. In Group A, several talked about how difficult it was for them to get past the disbelief that this young child had actually shot and killed a classmate, even though they were looking at the girl's body on the floor. This question allowed some of the participants who had said little to identify their personal reactions.

In Group A, the next question of "Where are you experiencing this the most in your body?" further helped to build a "shared connectedness" among participants, as each could easily relate their physical response to all that happened; many had similar reactions. Those unable to identify earlier reactions could relate to the physical reactions they were experiencing, which helped develop that "connectedness" with other members. The result was the same in the law enforcement group.

Time

Group A was completed in two hours while Group B ran an hour and a half. After a break, officers at the scene and the dispatchers returned for additional debriefing of the details and personal reactions which they did not wish to talk about in the larger group. This was very beneficial for those most exposed individuals. The most exposed members in the education group did not want to return. The offer was again made one week later with no reply. This was unfortunate, as we have found that, among the most exposed, many do need the smaller, more personal and thorough debriefing.

Summary

Two different groups using the same approach shared similar reactions, but also unique reactions. The law enforcement group was more a "family" than the education group which was comprised of different school district team members, county team members, and school personnel. Those most exposed in the law enforcement group were more open to additional debriefing; this was not the case with the education group members. The law enforcement group was one operating system, whereas, the education group were multiple systems which may have been more effectively helped if allowed to debrief separately. Despite the issues that prohibited a formal debriefing, the majority of members from both groups did express that the process was helpful.

Situations will continue that will not allow a formal debriefing to be conducted; yet some education and processing for survivors is still very helpful. Even though each situation will be unique structure remains important. The fact that debriefers went into each of these situations with predetermined questions and a structured opening was calming for the participants as well as the debriefers.

Ms. Trimble wrote after her debriefing, "It would have been a disaster had we not altered the 'debriefing' format and predetermined the questions we were going to ask. In order to minimize their anxiety and enhance my credibility with these officers, I was introduced by an officer who had worked with me in previous debriefings and acknowledged that my brother, a State Trooper, was one of the team members. I felt that it was critical, in my opening statements, to assure the participants that this was a structured and controlled procedure. The positive feedback we received following the session reinforced the vital importance of the debriefing.

"I continue to be amazed at how this process helps the participants relax and 'give in' to the grief and trauma. As they tell their stories, you can see the body language change as the process takes over. The healing has begun. What a rewarding feeling.

Appendix H
When Cognitive Interventions Fail with Children of Trauma: Memory, Learning, and Trauma Intervention

When Cognitive Interventions Fail with Children of Trauma: Memory, Learning, and Trauma Intervention

William Steele

Abstract: *Research supports that children exposed to violence (and other trauma inducing incidents) are at a greater risk for cognitive dysfunctions. The ability to attend, focus, retain and recall which are primary learning functions begins to diminish. The ability to process verbal information, identify and verbalize internal emotional experiences also suffer and negatively weaken a child's ability to communicate to others in a way that allows others to be helpful. (van der Kolk, 2006; Steele 2003; Steele and Raider 2001; VanDalen 2001; Perry, 2000; Morse and Wiley, 1997). In short it becomes difficult to help traumatized children using traditional cognitive processes. Sensory "implicit" interventions which can be provided in school or agency settings, can help restore cognitive functions in traumatized children.*

If one understands the state of arousal, the term used to identify the neurophysiological responses to trauma, one understands that a traumatized child's predominant processes will be in the sub cortical and limbic areas of the brain which deal with non-verbal information (Perry, 2008; Levine & Kline, 2008; LeDoux, 2000), not the neocortex area of the brain that involves reasoning, linear thinking, analysis, the ability to make sense of one's experience and to reorder that experience, when needed, in ways that are manageable. The child who is lingering or frozen in a state of arousal due to past or current trauma simply has difficulty reassigning or thinking things through (Roemer and Lebowitz, 1998).

These cognitive deficiencies, therefore, dictate the need for non-cognitive approaches to help children overcome or minimize the learning, emotional and behavioral problems they can experience due to failing cognitive processes resources resulting from traumatic arousal. To define an alternative to traditional cognitive approaches, we need to delineate between "explicit" and 'implicit" memory processes.

Memory has two functions "implicit" and "explicit". Explicit memory sometimes referred to as "declarative" memory refers to primary cognitive processes. In "explicit" memory we have access to language. We have words to describe what it is we are thinking and feeling. Explicit memory allows us to process information, to reason, to make sense of our experiences. Such cognitive processes help us cope.

Unfortunately, unless trained by the military or law enforcement to respond cognitively to threatening situations, the majority of children, even adults are going to respond or experience a trauma in "implicit" memory. In "implicit" memory there is no language. There simply are no words to describe or communicate what is being experienced. Position Emission Tomography or PET scans have found that trauma also creates changes in the Broca's area of the brain that lead to difficulties in identifying and verbalizing our experiences (Van Dalen, 2001), a process normally accessible via explicit memory processes. In implicit memory our senses contain the memory - what we see, what we hear, sensations of smell, touch and taste become the "implicit" containers of that experience (Rothchild, 2000).

If there is no language in "implicit" memory to help verbalize what that experience is like, how then is it defined and explained? It is defined through an implicit process referred to as "iconic symbolization" (Michaesu and Baettig, 1996). Iconic symbolization is the process of giving our experience a visual identity. Images are created to contain all the elements of that experience - what happened, our emotional reactions to it, the horror and terror of the experience. The trauma experience therefore is more easily communicated through imagery. "When a terrifying incident such as trauma is experienced and does not fit into a contextual memory, a new memory or dissociation is established" (van der Kolk, 1987, p. 289). When memory cannot be linked linguistically in a contextual framework, it remains at a symbolic levels for which there are no words to describe it. To retrieve that memory so it can be encoded, given a language, and then integrated into consciousness, it must be retrieved and externalized in its symbolic perceptual (iconic) form (Steele, 2003).

In order to access this experience we must therefore use "sensory" interventions that allow children the opportunity to actually make us witnesses to their experiences, to present us with their "iconic" representations, to give us the opportunity to see what they are now seeing as they look at themselves and the world around them following their exposure to a traumatic experience. In this sense "a picture is worth a thousand words". Drawings provide a representation of those "iconic" symbols that implicitly define what that experience was like for the child (Steele, Malchiodi & Kuban, 2008).

When one understands trauma as an "implicit" experience versus an "explicit" (cognitive) experience, it follows that drawing becomes an effective almost necessary avenue to help children release the horrid, terror filled "iconic" memories of their traumatic experiences. Bryers (1996) cited numerous studies that illustrated the use of drawing to help children access those traumatic memories and channel them into a trauma narrative, which could then be reworked explicitly (cognitively) in ways that became manageable for them. Magwaza, Killian, Peterson and Pillay (1993) achieved similar results with South African children exposed to community violence. Following 9/11, The World Trade Center Children's Mural Project was unveiled in March 19, 2002 and depicted over 3,100 portraits drawn by children. This drawing project "served to lessen feelings of isolation and helplessness felt among those children who had difficulty understanding (cognitively) the complexity of this tragedy (Berberian, Bryant and Landsberg, 2003)." These children could not "explicitly" communicate the many ways 9/11 impacted them but they could "implicitly" define it through then self-portraits.

Drawing is by no means a new vehicle for self-expression. Machooen (1949) many years ago noted the fact that the most expressive part of the body and the center of communication is one's face. Saigh (1999) suggested, "children prepare sketches of their stressful experience and verbally repeat (narrate) the content of their experience" (p. 370). Drawing does provide children with a focal point and an impetus to tell their story and to thereafter translate their experience into a narrative (Malchiodi, 1998). Riley (1997) indicated that the act of drawing is a form of externalization, a way for the children to put the experience outside themselves to make it real and concrete. Drawing is a way for that child to allow us to become a witness to what that experience was like by giving us a visual representation of the way they see it (Steele, 2008, 2003, 2001). Gil (2003) wrote when children draw, they do so on paper of specific physical dimensions with set boundaries. Once the images are placed on the space on the paper the child has in essence contained what might otherwise feel staggering. What might be experienced as disorganized or chaotic may then take on qualities of something that is manageable. Random thoughts and feelings might render children over stimulated and confused. Thoughts and feelings "shrunk down" enough to appear within specified dimensions may give children a sense of control (p. 156).

Drawings help children in the following ways (Steele and Raider, 2001):

- Drawing is a psychomotor activity that helps to trigger the sensory memories of the traumatic experience when it is trauma focused.
- Drawing provides a safe vehicle to communicate what children, even adults, often have few words to describe.
- Drawing engages the child/adult in active involvement in their own healing. It takes them from a passive to an active, directed, controlled externalization of that trauma experience.
- Drawing provides a symbolic representation of the trauma experience in a format that makes us a witness to the experience so we can now see what the child sees as he looks at himself and the world around him.
- Drawing provides a visual focus on details that encourage the client via trauma-specific questions, to tell his story, to give it a language so it can be reordered in a way that is manageable.
- Drawing also provides for the diminishing of reactivity (anxiety) to trauma memories through repeated visual reexposure in a medium that is perceived and felt by the client to be safe.
- Drawing helps the child externalize the experience, remove it to a safe container (chewing paper) outside himself.
- The drawing itself becomes a concrete representation the child can manipulate anyway needed to now feel power over it. The sensory memory of terror-feeling totally unsafe and powerless is replaced with the sensory experience of regaining power over it as well as feeling safe once

again as the experience is now contained and outside himself. He can experience putting distance between himself and the experience and thereby feeling safer.

However, to be helpful and safe, drawing activities must be structured and focused on the specific themes (experiences) of trauma such as, terror, hurt, worry, anger, and accountability. The telling of the story must be guarded by trauma specific questions that again help the child stay focused on the "themes" of experience. Once the child can put a story to his experience, the entire experience can then be encoded by "explicit" memory and thereafter reordered in ways the child can now manage, in ways that no longer trigger the fear, terror, worry, hurt, the absence of a sense of safety, the sense of being powerless. Once this is accomplished trauma symptoms begin to diminish (Steele and Raider, 2001; Malchiodi, 2003).

For more detailed decriptions of the use of drawing we recommend *Structured Sensory Interventions for Traumatized Children, Adolescents, and Parents.*

REFERENCES

Beyers, J. (1996), Children of the stones: Art therapy interventions in the West Bank. *Art Therapy: Journal of the American Art Therapy Association, 13,* 238-243.

Berberian, M., Bryant L., Landsburg, M., (2003) Interventions with Communities Affected by Mass Violence In Malchiodi, C., (Ed) *Handbook of Art Therapy,* New York, Guilford Publications.

LeDoux, I.E., Romanski, L. & Xagoraris, A., (1991), Indelibility of sub cortical emotional memories. *Journal of Cognitive Neuroscience, 1,* 238-243.

Magwaza, A., Killian, B. Peterson, I., & Pillay, Y. (1993). The effects of chronic stress on preschool children living in South African townships. *Child Abuse and Neglect, 17,* 795-803.

Malchiodi, C. (1998). *Understanding children's drawings.* New York: Guilford.

Malchiodi, C. (Ed) (2003). *Handbook of Art Therapy.* New York: Guilford.

Michaesu, G., & Baettig, D. (1996). An integrated model of posttraumatic stress disorder. *European Journal of Psychiatry, 10(4),* 243-245.

Perry, B. (2000). *Violence and childhood: How persisting fear can alter the developing child's brain.* The Child Trauma Academy. childtrauma@bcm.tmc.edu.

Riley, S. (1997). Children's art and narratives: An opportunity to enhance therapy and a supervisory challenge. *The Supervision Bulletin, 9,* 2-3.

Rothchild, B. (2000). *The body remembers.* New York: W.W. Norton.

Saigh, P., & Bremner, J. (1999) *Posttraumatic stress disorder.* Boston: Allyn and Bacon.

Starknum, P.A., Gebarski, M.N., Berent, S.S., & Schterngart, D.E. (Eds). (1992). Hippocampal formation volume, memory of dysfunction, and cortisol levels in patients with Cushing's syndrome. *Biology Psychiatry, 32,* 756-765.

Steele, W., & Raider, M. (2001). *Structured sensory intervention for children, adolescents, and parents (SITCAP).* New York: Mellen Press.

Steele, W., (2003). Helping Traumatized Children. In Straussner S., and Phillips, N. (Eds) *Understanding Mass Violence,* New York. Allyn and Bacon, 42-56.

vanDalen, A., (2001) Juvenile violence and addiction: Tangle roots in childhood trauma. *Journal of Social Work Practice in the Additions, I,* 25-40.

van der Kolk, B., McFarlane, A., & Weisaeth, L. (1996). (Eds.). *Traumatic stress disorder: The effects of overwhelming experience on mind, body, and society.* New York: Guilford.

Weinstein, D. (2000, Oct.). PTSD and ADHD. *ADHD Report, 8* (5).

Appendix I
References
TLC Institute Information

References

American Psychiatric Association. (1994). <u>Diagnostic and Statistical Manual of Mental Disorders (DSM-IV)</u> (4th ed.). Washington, D.C. American Psychiatric Association.

Armstrong, K., O'Callahan, W., & Marmar, C. (1991). Debriefing Red Cross disaster personnel: The Multiple Stressor Debriefing Model. <u>Journal of Traumatic Stress, 4,</u> 581-594.

Beyers, J. (1996). Children of the stones: Art therapy interventions in the West Bank. <u>Art Therapy: Journal of the American Art Therapy Association 13</u>, 238-243.

Everly, G., Mitchell, J. (2000). The debriefing "controversy" and crisis intervention: a review of ethical and substantive issues. <u>International Journal of Emergency Mental Health</u>. Vol. 2, Number 4, 211-225.

Griffin, C.A. (1987). Community disasters and PTSD: A debriefing model for response. In T. Williams (Eds.), <u>PTSD: A Handbook for Clinicians</u>. Cincinnati: American Disabled Veterans Publication.

Herman, J. (1992). <u>Trauma and Recovery,</u> New York, Basic Books.

Hobfoll, S.E., Briggs, S., & Wells, J. (1994). Community stress and resources: Actions and reactions. Paper presented at the NATO conference on stress, coping and disaster in Bonas, France.

Johnson, K. (1993). <u>School Crisis Management: A Hands-On Guide to Training Crisis Response Teams</u>. Alameda, CA, Hunter House,Inc., Publishers.

LeDoux, J.E. (2000). Emotion circuits in the brain. <u>Ann. Ped. Neurol. 23</u>: 155-184.

Levine, P. & Kline, M. (2008). <u>Trauma proofing your kids.</u> Berkley, California: North Atlantic Books.

Malchiodi, C. (2008). <u>Creative Interventions with Traumatized Children</u>. New York, Guilford Press.

Malchiodi, C.(1998). <u>Understanding Children's Drawings</u>. New York, Guilford Publishing Co.

McFarlane, A.C. (1994). Helping victims of disasters. In J.R. Freedy & S.E. Hobfoll (Eds.)., <u>Traumatic Stress:From Theory to Practice</u>. New York: Plenum.

Meichenbaum, D. (1994). <u>A Clinical Handbook/Practical Therapist Manual For Assessing and Treating Adults with Post-Traumatic Stress Disorder (PTSD).</u> Waterloo, Ontario, Canada, Institute Press.

Mitchell, J. (2004). *Crisis Intervention and CISM: A Research Summary.* www.icis.org/articles/cism_research_summary.pdf (8/04)

Pennebaker, J.W., & Harber, K.D. (1993). A social stage model of collective coping: The Lorna Prieta Earthquake and the Persian Gulf War. Journal of Social Issues, 49, 125-148.

Perry, B. & Szalavitz, M. (2007). The Boy Who Was Raised as a Dog: And Other Stories from a Child Psychiatrist's Notebook: What Traumatized Children Can Teach Us about Loss, Love, and Healing. New York, NY: Basic Books.

Peterson, S., & Straub, R. (1992). School Crisis Survival Guide. New York, The Center for Applied Research in Education.

Pynoos, R., & Nader, K. (1988). Psychological first aid and treatment approach to children exposed to community violence: research implications. Journal of Traumatic Stress 1, 445-473.

Pynoos, R., & Nader, K. (1990). Children exposed to violence and traumatic death. Psychiatric Annals 20, 334-344.

Raider, M., Santiago, A. & Steele, W. (1998) Trauma response kit: short-term trauma Intervention Model Evaluation, unpublished manuscript, Wayne State University.

Raphael, B. (1986). When Disaster Strikes: A Handbook for the Caring Professions. London: Hutchinson.

Raphael, B., & Wilson, J.P. (1994). When disaster strikes: Managing emotional reactions in rescue workers. In J.P. Wilson, & J.D. Lindy (Eds.). Countertransference in the Treatment of PTSD, New York: Guilford.

Roje, J. (1995). LA '94 Earthquake in the eyes of children: art therapy with elementary school children who were victims of disaster. Art Therapy Journal of the American Art Therapy Association 12, 237-243.

Saigh, P.A. (Ed.), (1992). Posttraumatic Stress Disorder: Behavioral Assessment and Treatment. Elmsford, N.Y.: Maxwell Press.

Shalev, A.Y. (1994) Debriefing following traumatic exposure. In R.J. Ursano et al. (Eds.). Trauma and Disaster. Cambridge: Cambridge University Press.

Solomon, S.D. (1992). Mobilizing social support networks in times of disaster. In C. Figley (Ed.), Trauma and it's Wake.II. New York: Brunner/Mazel.

Steele, W., & Raider, M. (2001). Structured sensory interventions for children, adolescents,and parents (SITCAP). New York, NY: Edwin Mellen Press.

Steele, W. & Trimble, T. (2001) Trauma debriefing: Structuring larger groups. <u>Trauma and Loss: Research and Interventions 1:2,</u> 10-12.

Steele, W. (1992). <u>Trauma Response Teams in Schools</u>. Detroit, Michigan: TLC Institute.

Steele, W., (1998). <u>Trauma Response Kit: Short-term Intervention Model</u>, Grosse Pointe, Michigan, TLC Institute.

Talbot, A., Manton, M., & Dunn, P.J. (1992). Debriefing the debriefers: An intervention strategy to assist psychologists after a crisis. <u>Journal of Traumatic Stress.</u> 5, 45-62.

Terr, L. (1991). Childhood traumas - An outline and overview. <u>American Journal of Psychiatry 148</u>, 10-20.

Turnbull, G.J. (1994). Acute treatments. In B. van der Kolk, S.M. Farlane, & L. Weisaeth (Eds.)., <u>PTSD handbook.</u> New York: Guilford.

van der Kolk, B. (2006) Clinical Implications of Neuroscience Research in PTSD. <u>Annals New York Academy of Sciences.</u> 1: 1-17.

van der Kolk, B., Roth, S., Pelcovitz, D. & Mandel, F. (1993). Complex posttraumatic stress Disorder: Results from the DSM-IV field trial of PTSD. In D. Meichenbaum. <u>A Clinical Handbook/Practical Therapist Manual: For Assessing and Treating Adults with Post-Traumatic Stress Disorder (PTSD)</u>, Waterloo, Ontario, Canada Institute Press.

Williams, C.M., Miller, J., Watson, G., & Hunt, N. (1994). A strategy for trauma debriefing after railway suicides. <u>Social Science and Medicine. 38</u>, 483-487.

Yule, W. & Udwin, O. (1991). Screening child survivors for post-traumatic stress disorders: Experiences from the "Jupiter" Sinking. <u>British Journal of Clinical Psychology 30</u>, 131-138.

Yule, W. (1992). Post-traumatic stress disorder in child survivors of shipping disasters: The sinking of the "Jupiter". <u>Psychotherapy and Psychosomatrics 57</u>, 200-205.

TLC On Site Trainings

TLC makes trauma training easily accessible to teachers, counselors, clergy, bereavement and hospice staff, marriage and family therapists, social workers, nurses, psychologists, and school administrators by conveniently completing the training at YOUR school or agency. TLC will work diligently to create a training that is specific to YOUR clientele and staff needs. In turn, your entire school or agency community will receive the same training at the same time, bringing everyone up to speed together. By completing the training in your town, your school or agency will save funds otherwise used for travel and out of town training costs. To schedule your TLC training, simply select a date and time convenient for your school or agency and call TLC at 877-306-5256 or email ckuban@tlcinst.org.

- ✔ Pick dates to fit your schedule
- ✔ Save on travel expenses and registration fees
- ✔ Entire staff will receive the SAME training at the SAME time
- ✔ Administrators are more likely to be able to attend a training at your site
- ✔ TLC can tailor trainings to focus on the areas of your greatest needs
- ✔ Able to train 25-250 participants at one time with no additional costs for larger groups

TLC Certified Trauma and Loss Specialists

Today there are 5,000 TLC Certified Trauma and Loss Specialists using TLC school and agency intervention programs supported by evidence based research. Table top activities, case examples, small group activities and video-taped segments provide for a multi-modal approach to learning and applying trauma specific strategies specific to school settings or agency/community settings. Upon completion, participants are well qualified and have access to the tools and resource materials to immediately initiate trauma specific strategies in their settings. Level One Certification can be completed by attending three days of core presentations followed by taking two online courses and one comprehensives essay exams thereby reducing time away from one's work setting. For more information about the TLC Certification Program, including Levels1, 2 and 3, call 1-877-306-5256 or email steele@tlcinst.org or go to tlcinstitute.org.

Benefits of TLC Certification

- ✔ National recognition for expertise in trauma
- ✔ Immediate access to TLC's National network of Certified practitioners, specialty areas, experience with special populations
- ✔ Inclusion, if appropriate in TLC's referral database
- ✔ Discounts on TLC trainings and resource materials.

- ✔ Consultation with TLC staff
- ✔ Access to TLC's online journal
- ✔ Eligible for Level-2 and Level-3 Certification
- ✔ Opportunities to participate in special projects and research
- ✔ Eligible to present at TLC's annual Childhood Trauma Practitioners Assembly

TLC Courses & Credits

TLC offers courses designed to enable schools, crisis teams, child and family counselors, and private practitioners to help traumatized children. Online courses are also available.

- ✔ Children of Trauma
- ✔ Structured Sensory Intervention
- ✔ Trauma Debriefing
- ✔ Crisis Intervention
- ✔ Suicide Intervention
- ✔ Adolescent Grief

- ✔ Art, Play Interventions
- ✔ Understanding Children's Drawings
- ✔ Psycho-Physiology of Trauma
- ✔ Managing & Discharging Activation
- ✔ Reaching & Teaching Stressed Students
- ✔ Supporting Students with Special Needs

Professional CEs Include (partial list)**:** American Psychological Association (APA), National Board for Certified Counselors (NBCC), The Association for Play Therapy, (APT-only for courses with 'Play' in title), National Association of Social Workers (NASW) Michigan Nurses Association (MNA),University of San Diego Graduate Extension Level Credit, Grand Valley State University Graduate Credit. For a complete list of credits available go to tlcinstitute.org.

TLC Online Courses

All courses provide professional CEs, some include books. Go to www.tlcinstitute.org for more information.

- ✔ Adolescent Grief
- ✔ Suicide Intervention
- ✔ Working Through an Ethical Lens
- ✔ Trauma Informed Schools
- ✔ Zero to Three: Trauma Intervention
- ✔ Domestic Violence

- ✔ Eating Disorders and Trauma
- ✔ Pain Management
- ✔ Psycho-Physiology of Trauma
- ✔ Resilience and Posttraumatic Growth in Children
- ✔ Art, Play, Music, Drama & Bibliotherapy
- ✔ Reaching and Teaching Stressed and Anxious Students

THE NATIONAL INSTITUTE
FOR TRAUMA AND LOSS
IN CHILDREN

STARR
COMMONWEALTH

A STARR INSTITUTE   INSTITUTE
FOR TRAINING PROGRAM   FOR TRAINING

Tools to Help the Helper

TLC's Resources for Infants, Children, Adolescents & Parents

Handbook of Trauma Interventions: Zero to Three
by Caelan Kuban

Contains current information & research on how trauma impacts infant brain development. Provides interventions to work with infants, toddlers, parents & caregivers who have experienced a trauma or loss. Included are tools to help educate parents and caregivers, facilitate secure attachments, and reduce trauma-induced arousal reactions so that healing can occur. **Ages 0-3**

● ● ● ● ● ● ● ● ● ● ● ● ● ● ● ● ● ● **$20**

Raising Resilient Children in a Traumatic World: A Guide For Parents From Parents
by Caelan Kuban and William Steele

NEW in 2009! What allows some traumatized children to do better than others? TLC's qualitative research with traumatized school aged children resulted in this new resource to be used with parents and children. For research outcomes go to tlcinstitute.org. **Ages 6-12 and Parents**

● ● ● ● ● ● ● ● ● ● ● ● ● ● ● ● ● ● **$25**

A Time for Resilience: Helping Children Become Resilient in a Traumatic World
by Caelan Kuban and William Steele

NEW in 2009! TLC's qualitative research with traumatized school aged children resulted in this new program for professionals to use with parents, children, individually, in the classroom, or as an after school program. For research outcomes go to tlcinstitute.org. Includes the book *Raising Reslient Children in a Traumatic World.* **Ages 6-12 and Parents**

● ● ● ● ● ● ● ● ● ● ● ● ● ● ● ● ● ● **$55**

Brave Bart: A Story for Traumatized and Grieving Children
by Caroline Sheppard and Illustrated by John Manikoff

Brave Bart is a kitty who had something bad, sad and scary happen to him. Helping Hannah, a neighborhood cat, helps Bart overcome his fears and become a survivor. *Brave Bart* normalizes many trauma-reactions children experience. Parents find it an excellent way to talk to and comfort their traumatized child. **Ages 4-10**

● ● ● ● ● ● ● ● ● ● ● ● ● ● ● ● ● ● **$15**

Also available on DVD for $20/ea

You Are Not Alone, A Trauma is Like No Other Experience and, What Parents Need to Know
by William Steele

You Are Not Alone lets traumatized children know that they are not alone. Helps children define trauma, understand reactions, and find ways to heal the hurt. **Ages 6-12**
A Trauma is Like No Other Experience was written especially for teens and addresses being a victim, seeing a trauma, and knowing someone who was victimized. Addresses reactions and actions that follow a traumatizing event. **Ages: 13-18**
What Parents Need to Know provides parents with the basis of understanding children who have experienced a trauma, and directs the parents on the journey of helping their children heal. **Ages: Adult**

● ● ● ● ● ● ● ● ● ● ● ● **$5 ea or 3/$12**

Helping Children Feel Safe
by William Steele, Cathy Malchiodi & Nancy Klein

Provides professionals with a series of sensory-based activities designed to help children who have experienced a trauma to re-establish a sense of safety. Helps to debrief and defuse. Buy the book alone or the entire program which includes the TLC books, *Brave Bart, Debriefing Handbook,* and *What Parents Need to Know.* **Ages 6-10**

● ● ● ● Book only $50 or Complete Program $105

One-Minute Trauma Interventions for Children and Adolescents
by Caelan Kuban and William Steele

NEW in 2008! A collection of age-specific, sensory-based trauma intervention activities that focus on the major themes of trauma. Designed especially for use with children and adolescents in school and agency settings when time is limited. All intervention activities take less than 20 minutes to complete. **Ages 3-18**

● **$50**

After a Traumatic Loss
by William Steele

An excellent reference for those who work with grieving children. The book identifies differences between grief and trauma and describes reactions that children often experience. **Ages 6+**

● ● ● ● ● ● ● ● ● ● ● ● ● ● ● ● ● ● **$8**

Trauma Intervention Program for Children and Adolescents
by William Steele

REVISED in 2009! TLC's most comprehensive program, *Trauma Intervention Program,* provides 8-sessions of structured, sensory interventions for children and adolescents and a component for parents of traumatized children.. Researched in school & agency settings it has been shown to significantly reduce trauma reactions. Included are 2 manuals, 2 workbooks, 3 booklets and a DVD which includes *You Are Not Alone, A Trauma is Like No Other Experience,* and *What Parents Need to Know,* Assessment tools, and other supportive materials. **Ages: 6-18**

● ● ● ● ● ● ● ● ● ● ● ● ● ● ● ● ● ●**$145**

I Feel Better Now! Trauma Intervention Program
by William Steele, Pamela Lemerand
Deanne Ginns-Gruenberg & Caelan Kuban

REVISED This 10-session, evidence-based researched, group program for children addresses violent or non-violent trauma. The group process is based on an educational model of teaching, exploring, guiding, normalizing and reframing experiences. *Leaders Guide, Workbook, Don't Pop Your Cork on Monday* and the TLC booklets, *You Are Not Alone and What Parents Need to Know* are included. Go to www.tlcinst.org for research outcomes. **Ages 6-12**

● ● ● ● ● ● ● ● ● ● ● ● ● ● ● ● ● ●**$105**

What Color Is Your Hurt? Trauma Intervention Program
by William Steele

This 10-session program has been shown to help preschool children find relief from trauma. Included is an *Intervention Manual* for the professional, an *Activity Workbook, Brave Bart* storybook and, *What Parents Need to Know.* **Ages 3-6**

● ● ● ● ● ● ● ● ● ● ● ● ● ● ● ● ● ●**$105**

Adults and Parents in Trauma: Learning to Survive Trauma Intervention Program
by William Steele

Included are 2 manuals and workbooks, one for parents of a traumatized child, and one for adults or parents who have experienced a personal trauma at some time. It contains assessment tools, checklists, cognitive reframing statements, healing benchmarks, secondary victimization, survivor plan, worry activities, survivor activities. Also included is the TLC, *After the Violence* video. **Ages: Adult**

● ● ● ● ● ● ● ● ● ● ● ● ● ● ● ● ● ●**$105**

SITCAP: At-Risk Adjudicated Treatment Program (SITCAP-ART)
by William Steele & Jacqueline Jacobs

Structured Sensory Interventions for Traumatized Children, Adolescents and Parents: At-Risk Adjudicated Treatment Program (SITCAP-ART) is an evidence-based researched, group program for at risk or adjudicated youth in outpatient or residential settings. TLC research of SITCAP-ART supports reductions in PTSD symptoms, rule breaking behavior, aggressive behavior and other mental health symptoms. Designed for adolescents ages 13-18, it consists of 10 sessions and provides Juvenile Justice programs with an effective trauma-specific intervention. Go to www.tlcinst.org for research outcomes. Includes manual and workbook. **Ages 13-18**

● ● ● ● ● ● ● ● ● ● ● ● ● ● ● ● ● ●**$125**

Structured Sensory Intervention for Traumatized Children, Adolescents and Parents (SITCAP)
by William Steele & Melvyn Raider

This textbook discusses a comprehensive treatment approach to treating trauma victims. Gives detailed descriptions of interventions, case studies, answers to common therapeutic struggles. Quantitative, qualitative, and case-oriented data. Beneficial for professional development and graduate level training. **Level: Professional**

● ● ● ● ● ● ● ● ● ● ● ● ● ● ● ● ● ●**$30**

Trauma Informed Care: 50 Frequently Asked Questions about Trauma Intervention
by Caelan Kuban and William Steele

A "go-to" guide for new and experienced clinicians. Includes answers to the most commonly asked questions about specific trauma interventions and provides trauma informed care directives. **Level: Professional**

● ● ● ● ● ● ● ● ● ● ● ● ● ● ● ● ● ●**$15**

Children of Trauma: Tools to Help the Helper (DVD)
TLC's Structured Sensory Intervention is used in 3 case studies. Children are interviewed, demonstrating specific trauma intervention tasks and questions. 60 min, **Level: Professional**
After the Violence (VHS) Parents of children who died violently and traumatically tell their story. Survivors identify specific reactions and talk about the healing process. 60 min, **Level: Professional**
Schools Response to Terrorism (VHS) An informative and powerful presentation by NYC School Personnel about their experiences on 9/11/2001 and the weeks that followed. 120 min, **Level: Professional**

● ● ● ● ● ● ● ● ● ● ● ● ● ● ● ● ● ●**$45/ea**

A Handbook of Interventions Following Suicide or Trauma in Schools
by William Steele

This handbook details interventions specific to the suicidal student, as well as for the trauma experienced by the survivors. An invaluable tool which includes assessment of risk, scripted responses, checklists, legal responsibilities, emergency referral procedures and resource materials. **Level: School professional**

• $30

Trauma Debriefing Handbook for Schools and Agencies
by William Steele

This handbook includes strategies that have been field-tested by hundreds of TLC Certified Trauma and Loss Specialists and Consultants. It provides detailed step-by-step debriefing protocol, as well as five debriefing models for: K-5th grade, classrooms, adults, staff, and crisis team members. Buy the book alone or with a 25-minute demonstration video. **Level: Professional**

• • • • • • • **Book & DVD $60 or Book Only $30**

Trauma Response Protocol Manual
by William Steele, Marie Nelson, Patti Porter, Dee Ingle, Paul Brohl, & Noreen Brohl

REVISED! Includes: standardized Protocol Manual, straight-forward task list for quick reference, and multiple letters and handouts ready for last minute duplication. Emergency Response Protocol Quick Reference Guide is designed to be kept in classrooms. It is an abbreviated set of protocol for staff. **Level: School professional**

• • • • • • • • • • • • • • • • • • $75

Supporting Students with Special Needs
by Jean Cooper, Tracy Bullock & William Steele

This manual presents baseline behaviors of the varied impairments, as well as the changes in these behaviors when these children are exposed to grief or trauma. Included are interventions that address emotional, cognitive, and behavioral needs. Specific interventions for special education teachers, and parents of special needs students. **Level: School professional**

• $45

TLC's PTSD Child and Adolescent Questionnaire (CAQ)

Excellent, age-specific pre and post intervention assessment tool. Helps to identify the frequency of occurrence of trauma reactions by sub-category as classified by the DSM-IVR; avoidance, re-experiencing and arousal. The CAQ has achieved convergent validity with Briere's Trauma Symptom Child Checklist. Pack of 10 Child OR Adolescent OR 5 of each. Please specify when ordering. **Ages: Children 6-12/Adolescents 13-18**

• $20

TLC Online Journal
Trauma and Loss: Research and Interventions

TLC's Online Journal is published twice yearly. The Journal is available on the TLC website. Articles, commentaries, book reviews, and more. **Level: Professional**

Parents Trauma Resource Center

Free resources are available on the TLC website for professionals who work with traumatized children and their parents. The web site is translated into three languages: English, Spanish and Arabic. Information, activities, handouts and worksheets to download. This is a valuable resource for professionals and parents alike. Go to the TLC web site at www.tlcinstitute.org and click on the Parent Trauma Resource Center link. **Level: Professional, Parents**

TLC Online Courses

All courses provide professional CEs, some include books. Go to www.tlcinstitute.org for more information.

- ✔ Adolescent Grief
- ✔ Suicide Intervention
- ✔ Working Through an Ethical Lens
- ✔ Trauma Informed Schools
- ✔ Zero to Three: Trauma Intervention
- ✔ Domestic Violence

- ✔ Eating Disorders and Trauma
- ✔ Pain Management
- ✔ Psycho-Physiology of Trauma
- ✔ Resilience and Posttraumatic Growth in Children
- ✔ Art, Play, Music, Drama & Bibliotherapy
- ✔ Reaching and Teaching Stressed and Anxious Students

Order Form

ITEM	PRICE	QTY	TOTAL
Adults & Parents in Trauma Program	$105		
After a Traumatic Loss	$8		
After the Violence Video	$45		
A Trauma Is Like No Other Experience	$5		
A Time for Resilience Program	$55		
Brave Bart Storybook	$15		
Children of Trauma: Tools to Help the Helper DVD	$45		
Handbook of Suicide Interventions	$30		
Handbook of Trauma Interventions: Zero to Three	$20		
Helping Children Feel Safe Book Only	$50		
Helping Children Feel Safe Program	$105		
I Feel Better Now! Program	$105		
Interventions for Students with Special Needs	$45		
One-Minute Interventions	$50		
PTSD Child Questionnaire (pack of 10)	$20		
PTSD Adolescent Questionnaire (pack of 10)	$20		
PTSD Child & Adolescent Questionnaire (pack of 5 ea)	$20		
Raising Resilient Children in a Traumatic World	$25		
Schools Response to Terrorism video	$45		
SITCAP-ART Intervention Program	$125		
SITCAP Interventions Textbook	$30		
Three TLC Booklets	$12		
Three TLC Booklets on DVD	$20		
Trauma and Loss Journal subscription (email required)	$40		
Trauma Debriefing Handbook & DVD	$60		
Trauma Debriefing Handbook only	$30		
Trauma Informed Care: 50 Frequently Asked Questions	$15		
Trauma Intervention Program	$145		
Trauma Protocol Manual w/Staff Manual	$75		
What Color Is Your Hurt? Program	$105		
What Parents Need to Know	$5		
You Are Not Alone	$5		
	SUB-TOTAL		
	Shipping & Handling		
	TOTAL AMOUNT DUE		

MAIL:

TLC Institute,
900 Cook Road
Grosse Pointe Woods,
Michigan 48236

FAX: 313-885-1861

PHONE: 877-306-5256

ORDER ONLINE:

www.tlcinstitute.org

click on the link
to enter the online store

Call TLC at 877-306-5256 for discounts and S&H prices for large orders, special delivery rates, and for shipping to Alaska,

Shipping & Handling	
0-$25	+ $5.95
$26-$50	+ $10.95
$51-$115	+ $13.95
$116-$200	+ $16.95
$201-$400	+ $26.95
Over $400	– Call for price

Hawaii and outside the US. Please be advised that the shipping amount is an estimate only. Actual charges will be calculated at time of shipping and will be added to your total. Prices listed are subject to change.

Please use this code when ordering
END OF BOOKS

Name_____

Organization _____

Address _____

City/State/Zip_____

Day Phone _____ Email _____

☐ I have enclosed a Purchase Order   ☐ Check enclosed (payable to TLC)   ☐ Pay by Credit Card   ☐ MasterCard   ☐ VISA

Credit card number   Expiration date   CVV on back of card